LOVE
AND
SEXUALITY

Translation from the French
original title : L'AMOUR ET LA SEXUALITÉ *

Omraam Mikhaël Aïvanhov

LOVE
AND
SEXUALITY

Part 1

3rd edition

Complete Works — Volume 14

EDITIONS PROSVETA

Editor-Distributor

Editions PROSVETA S.A. – B.P. 12 – 83601 Fréjus Cedex (France)

Distributors

AUSTRIA
MANDALA
Verlagsauslieferung für Esoterik
A-6094 Axams, Innsbruckstraße 7

BELGIUM
PROSVETA BENELUX
Van Putlei 105 B-2548 Lint

N.V. MAKLU Somersstraat 13-15
B-2000 Antwerpen

VANDER S.A.
Av. des Volontaires 321
B-1150 Bruxelles

BRAZIL
NOBEL SA
Rua da Balsa, 559
CEP 02910 - São Paulo, SP

BRITISH ISLES
PROSVETA Ltd
The Doves Nest
Duddleswell Uckfield,
East Sussex TN 22 3JJ

Trade orders to :
ELEMENT Books Ltd
Unit 25 Longmead Shaftesbury
Dorset SP7 8PL

CANADA
PROSVETA Inc.
1565 Montée Masson
Duvernay est, Laval, Que. H7E 4P2

GERMANY
URANIA – Rudolf-Diesel-Ring 26
D-8029 Sauerlach

HOLLAND
STICHTING
PROSVETA NEDERLAND
Zeestraat 50
2042 LC Zandvoort

HONG KONG
HELIOS – J. Ryan
P.O. BOX 8503
General Post Office, Hong Kong

IRELAND
PROSVETA IRL.
84 Irishtown – Clonmel

ITALY
PROSVETA Coop. a r.l.
Cas. post. 13046 – 20130 Milano

LUXEMBOURG
PROSVETA BENELUX
Van Putlei 105 B-2548 Lint

NORWAY
PROSVETA NORDEN
Postboks 5101
1501 Moss

PORTUGAL
PUBLICAÇÕES
EUROPA-AMERICA Ltd
Est Lisboa-Sintra KM 14
2726 Mem Martins Codex

SPAIN
ASOCIACIÓN PROSVETA ESPAÑOLA
C/ Ausias March n° 23 Principal
SP-08010 Barcelona

SWITZERLAND
PROSVETA
Société Coopérative
CH - 1808 Les Monts-de-Corsier

UNITED STATES
PROSVETA U.S.A.
P.O. Box 49614
Los Angeles, California 90049

VENEZUELA
J.P. Leroy
Apartado 51 745
Sabana Grande
1050 A – Caracas

Editions Prosveta S.A. – B.P. 12 – 83601 Fréjus Cedex (France)

ISBN 2-85566-423-3

édition originale : ISBN 2-85566-311-3

By the same author
(translated from the French)

'Complete Works' Collection

Brochures :

New Presentation

Omraam Mikhaël Aïvanhov

Contents

Foreword

The reader should know that this book is intended for those who are searching for a means of advancing spiritually. Everything seems to have already been written on the subject of love and sexuality, for poets and novelists have described the joys and sorrows of lovers, and philosophers have for years debated the origin of the force which pushes people irresistibly towards each other, whilst biologists and psychologists have studied the sexual function, and doctors and psychiatrists have studied the symptoms of sexual malfunction. Moralists, both laymen and clergymen, have tried to contain the outpouring torrents of instinct and emotion with all kinds of taboos, whilst others ask for nothing more than to be carried away by them, experiencing every sensation and studying every technique.

Everything seems to have been already said, except this: that each human being has this force within him to help him evolve, to enable him to reach new heights. Men and women don't really know what it is that draws them to each other. But they constantly seek this attraction having discovered that one of their greatest sources of pleasure lies in the satisfaction of the sexual instinct. Even if the majority of their experiences end in failure, it never occurs to them that the reason for their failure lies in their incorrect understanding of love and sexuality. It is as though mankind has always accepted the fact that love is fatal, that it always starts out as a beautiful dream of perfect happiness and always ends in disillusionment or ruin. They do not err, however, in continuing to have hope, because it is true that only love can bring real happiness. Their disappointment is due to their not knowing how to live their love according to the science of the Initiates.

The Initiates teach that both man and woman are reflections of the divine principles that created the universe, the Eternal masculine principle and the Eternal feminine principle, and that man and woman also have the power to create. The union of man and woman, like the union of spirit and matter, can create worlds. But for their union to be so powerful, they must adopt a new form of love, a new understanding of love. They must know rules and methods, which despite all the literature on Tibetan tantrism, have never before been revealed. The ideas set forth in this volume may surprise and shock the reader for they are contrary to his present beliefs and ideas. But if he is really in search of spiritual advancement, he will learn how love will enable him to fulfil his divine predestination.

*The reader will better understand certain aspects
of the lectures published in the present volume
if he bears in mind that Master Omraam Mikhaël Aïvanhov's
Teaching was exclusively oral.*

Chapter I

The Masculine and Feminine Principles – The Love of God, The Love of Others, Self-Love

In the universe, there exist two essential principles which are reflected in every manifestation of life and Nature. All creation is the result of these two principles which are called, for the sake of convenience, the masculine and the feminine principles. These are reflections, repetitions of the two great divine principles which created everything, the Heavenly Father and the Divine Mother, who are the polarization of the unique principle, the Absolute, the Non-Manifest, which the Kabbalah calls Aïn Soph Aur. It is said that man was created in the image of God, that is, in the image of these two principles, the masculine and the feminine, one that is visible, and the other that is hidden, it is there, but it cannot be seen. Each woman is feminine on the outside and has within her the masculine principle and each man is masculine on the outside and has the feminine principle within. If you know this law of polarity and how to use the two principles, masculine and feminine, emissive and receptive, positive and negative, how many of your problems will then be resolved!

The two principles are in each one of us and can be seen everywhere, on the face, the body, the hands, in Nature, on flowers and fruit, mountains and rivers, in caves and among the stars. Wherever you look, on the earth, under or above it, from the bottom of the ocean to the highest sky, you will find one or the other principle, in one form or another.

Consciously or unconsciously, all creatures react the same way

to this question of the two principles; for every creature it is of
absolute importance, nothing counts but these two principles.
When a man is looking for a wife to marry, he is ready to
abandon everything, a king is ready to leave his kingdom and his
subjects, his army and his treasure, for the sake of a wife . . . What
is it about a woman that makes an entire nation of men turn
pale? Actually, it is the principle, not the woman herself, that
man is seeking, for there is nothing higher than this principle.
You see, man is faithful, he seeks the principle, and he discards
whatever is not the principle. A woman does the same thing. She
stands up to her whole family, against the entire world, for the
man she loves. Why? Is she wrong? Not at all. It is God and
Mother Nature who have inscribed in the human heart: "Thou
shalt leave thy mother and thy father and follow thy wife (or
husband)." In the heart of each creature it is written that the first
principle should seek the second, and the second should seek the
first. Humans are not always conscious of this because the search
takes different forms depending upon whether the field is science,
philosophy, art, or religion.

Mystics claim that they seek God. Actually, what they think
of as God is the other part of themselves with which they seek
to unite, to become complete and perfect. Until then, they know
themselves to be divided, mutilated beings. All beings seek their
complementary principle which is called, in the science of the
Initiates, the twin-soul, there to find plenitude, peace,
omniscience, all-powerfulness, and become like the Lord. Only
the form varies.

Think about this question. Love contains everything, and
outside of love is a void and everlasting nothingness. The
religious, the puritans, the hypocrites don't admit it, but in
reality, they too are searching for love. They don't show it,
because they choose to obey the old laws of chastity, but Nature
doesn't recognize these human inventions, she works within each
being, making everything boil, blaze and burn. The question is to
know how to find love exactly as God understands it and then to

manifest it in accordance with divine laws, to come at last to fusion with the twin-soul.

The two principles are everywhere: when you eat and drink, when you look at someone or listen to them, when you work and even when you are singing here in this chorus . . . Yes, but you don't know what happens when you sing. The high notes of the sisters' voices, the brothers' deep and solemn tones, do you think that they vanish, lost in space? No, although you are unaware of it, their voices mingle somewhere overhead, and then send back something marvellous and divine. Your voice is impregnated with your magnetism, your vitality, your perfume. You are tied to your voice as if it were a little kite at the end of a long string. Your voice leaves you and goes flying above where it meets other voices with which to unite. Because of their singing, there is a delicate and divine exchange between the brothers and sisters, who thus receive the etheric elements they would not otherwise receive, except in much more primitive ways. In this delicate interchange of voices, our souls and spirits nourish themselves with what they have received, and at the same time they hand a few crumbs to the physical body, so that it won't starve to death.

When we sing, it is not until the two principles have done their creative work above that these creations can reach us through our ears, and that we benefit from a chaste exchange that is also divine. There can be no reproach for breaking the laws of purity, yet all are nourished and strengthened. This is why the habit of singing together has existed since the world began. Now that we no longer have the light and knowledge of the Initiates, we no longer know why we sing together, nothing remains but the exercise, men and women continue to sing together in chorus, country-folk sing and dance and are happy, because without realizing it their souls and spirits are communicating through the music and songs, and they receive in that way something that makes them feel relaxed and filled with joy for a while.

There are hundreds and thousands of methods which nature
has invented to permit humans to make exchanges when they are
unable to do so physically, there are swimming pools, beaches,
dances and even churches! Of course we are not told whether
these exchanges are orthodox or not, regardless of whether the
church is catholic or protestant or orthodox! A boy sees an
attractive girl in the street and follows her . . . into a church . . .
"Oh! he thinks, if it were a dance hall, I'd feel more like
following her . . ." but he follows her anyway into the church.
Aware that he has followed her, she puts on a few poses and
mannerisms, while he, instead of watching the priest and
following the service, stares at her as much as he dares. You see,
exchanges are made even in churches, delicate exchanges, but
what the two of them have in the back of their heads, no one can
say whether it is orthodox or unorthodox!

To return to the subject of singing. If you haven't a mouth you
are unable either to speak or to sing. The word, the song, depend
on the masculine and feminine principles which are the tongue
and the lips. You say that I am speaking scandalously, making
indelicate allusions. No, I am simply making a statement, it is
Nature, not I, who invented the mouth. To speak a word, the
tongue and lips have to go to work, otherwise, not a word, no
speech, no song will be released. A song, a word, are the result of
something: the children of a father and mother who are more
evolved and spiritual, since God has placed them in the head.
The tongue and lips have the same function as the sexual organs
since they are able to create, but they create in the spiritual
sphere: "In the beginning was the Word" . . . If we really want to
find the two principles, we must look above, not below; below,
the organs of men and women are nothing but a repetition, the
coarse reflection of the two principles above, which are also
creators, and which can give life exactly as do the two principles
below.

There, dear brothers and sisters, these few words were to show you the importance of songs, especially spiritual ones such as the mystic songs you sing here. Until now, singing was for you merely a pastime or a distraction. But now you must understand that it is a nourishment, a necessity, a spiritual need. If you don't know how to nourish yourself with music and song, the less subtle and delicate exchanges that you will make instead will bring you nothing but regret and bitterness.

This is a question that nobody understands. The mystics, hermits and ascetics who were so terribly ignorant and narrow as to destroy their equilibrium, health, and happiness by refusing all exchanges, became dried up corpses, lifeless and barren, unable to bear fruit, nothing. And of course, according to them, they were doing the will of the Lord. As if the Lord were in favor of death and corpses! The Lord is for life, for creativeness, that is all He does, create. It is humans who have reversed things by imagining that the Lord is against love, against marriage, against children. They believe this should be the pious life of the truly religious. What an odd religion!

You will say: "Most of the great Masters and Initiates never married, were they like those fanatics?" No, the great Masters and the Initiates were liberal, they understood God's creation, they saw things clearly. If they lived a pure and chaste life it was because the exchanges they made on the higher planes were so rich and marvellous that they didn't need to encumber themselves with matter. They lived a life of celibacy and chastity not because they were against love, on the contrary, they nourished themselves and drank from sources in regions unknown to the rest of the world, where the exchanges are made in the brightest light and in the greatest purity . . . They were in the midst of angels and Archangels, the sun and all the stars smiled on them and even humans gave them their love and trust, they were filled to overflowing with love from all sides! What else could they need? Why give up all those wonders for the sad disappointments of the swamps below? You may not understand me now, but you will.

It is said in the Gospels: "Thou shalt love the Lord thy God, with all thy heart, with all thy soul, and with all thy mind, and with all thy spirit, and thy neighbour as thyself." You see: love the Lord and love your neighbour. Nowhere does it say to love oneself. And yet what happens? Human beings love themselves first of all, and give what is left over to their fellow beings. As for the Lord, once a year they go to church and light a candle. Why is this? Nowhere does it say to love yourself, and yet that is all they do, and there is no time left for the other two commandments that are mentioned. Initiates have never said that one must love oneself because they know that the most natural tendency, the most tenacious and unalterable impulse of all is to love oneself, to satisfy oneself, to eat and drink and take everything, even that which belongs to someone else . . . The love of self, that is all one sees, night and day. And yet, actually, by saying to love the Lord and to love one's fellow beings, the Initiates were really saying: "Love thyself." They knew they would never be understood if they said it, but that is what they meant.

The love of self, the love of fellow creatures and the love of God: these three forms of love correspond to three stages in the life of man. The child loves only himself, he can think of no one else. Later on, he begins to love his father and mother, his brothers and sisters, his friends, and then his wife and children . . . Finally, deceived and betrayed by people, he turns to God, seeking only Him, loving only Him. Actually, I can show you that the higher degrees of love are contained in the love of self, for by loving others and loving God, it is really oneself that one loves, with a love that is finer and brighter and more spiritual, but it is the self that one loves, always. Why is it that you love one woman and not all women? Because this woman reflects something that is in you, and it is this reflection that is your other side, the other half of yourself. The human being is polarized, and this polarization pushes him into looking for the other part of himself through women or through men, and even through the Lord. It is always himself that he is seeking, himself that he loves, but not as he sees himself in the mirror, no. He seeks the other principle, the other pole. If you are a man, the other pole is a feminine principle, if you are a woman, it will be a masculine principle.

The human being, such as he is understood by the Initiates, is a complete being. The two poles, one positive and one negative, are the two halves of one unity which has become divided in the course of evolution. Originally, the human being was androgynous, both man and woman. When there occurred a separation of the sexes, each went its way, but each principle carries within it the imprint, the image of the other deeply engraved on his or her soul. This is why, when a man sees a face among hundreds and thousands of women, one face that reminds him of the image he carries in him, he leaps for joy and does everything possible to seek and find this woman. Unfortunately, after a while, he sees that these two images do not correspond, and he abandons that one to go looking for another, always in the hope that this time he will have found his other half, his twin-soul. It is as true for men as it is for women, there are no exceptions. But one day this meeting between the two principles will have to take place, because the love between the two principles is more powerful than anything.

Actually, our twin-soul is ourselves, the other pole of ourselves. We are below, and the other pole is above, allowing us to communicate with Heaven, with the angels, with God Himself, in perfection and plenitude. This is why, in all the Initiations, disciples were taught to find their other pole. In India, Jnana-yoga teaches the method by which the yogi can unite with his higher Self, and by so doing, he becomes united with God Himself. In Greece, the same idea is expressed in the formula written over the temple of Delphi: "Know thyself". It doesn't mean to know our character, good or bad, our qualities and faults, no, that would be too simple. In the Book of Genesis it says: "And Adam knew Eve" . . . "Abraham knew Sarah" . . . To know was a fusion of the two principles. "Know thyself" means:

find the other pole in yourself and become a divinity. If you are man, the other pole is woman, and you will know her as a lover knows his beloved ... Not in exactly the same way of course, because this fusion, this knowing takes place in the more luminous spheres of light. It is when you have penetrated into this light that you will become one with yourself.

We find the same precept expressed slightly differently in the Gospels: "Thou shalt love the Lord thy God, with all thy heart, with all thy soul, with all thy strength", which tells us that only through our higher Self can we communicate with God. It is also what Christ meant when he said: "No one cometh unto the Father save by me." The Christ is the symbol of Divinity, of the Word, he is the Son of God, the divine spark buried deep in every soul. By binding himself to his higher soul man becomes bound to the Christ principle which is everywhere, in every soul, and through Christ, he is bound to God. Only with your higher ego can you approach God, since it represents the best and the truest in you. This is the reason, when we meditate, that we must leave the physical world of matter far behind and rise to the luminous world above to attain the divine principle of our superior soul. In this way, because of the existing polarization, an affinity is created, a sympathy, a link with the complementary principle, the masculine being drawn to the feminine and the feminine to the masculine.

Everyone has his complementary principle within him, and can only reach God through this other principle. Woman finds God through man, because man represents the other principle, and this other principle connects her with the Heavenly Father. And man finds God through the feminine principle, whether through a woman, or through Nature which is a feminine principle, or through the Divine Mother. But without the feminine principle, there can be nothing, no forward impulse, no inspiration, no work done, nothing. And without the presence of the masculine principle, the feminine principle remains unformed and shapeless, inert, sterile. Go and study Nature's way of doing things, and you will see that the sun which is the masculine principle, projects light, heat, and life. In our inner life also, we must be fertilized, animated, vivified by the divine principle of the sun. It is easier for women because they are already receptive, but men, who are positive and emissive, have to change their polarization to become receptive.

Let us come back to the three degrees of love I was talking about. When you think about it, you realize that humans really don't know how to love themselves, they are more apt to destroy themselves. Is it loving to eat and drink no matter what, to smoke and to indulge in all kinds of folly? Are you being kind to yourself when you let anger or hatred take you over? No, you are poisoning yourself. You say: "But I want to poison so and so." Very well, but this poison must first pass through you before it can get out and poison the other person. Thus, you will be poisoned before him! You see, how much ignorance and what lack of understanding. We don't know how to love ourselves, and now we must learn how to love ourselves correctly.

Suppose that you wish nothing impure to get inside. Now, yes, you are being loving, because by your purity, you are preparing the magnificent conditions that will make it possible for the angels to come and install themselves within. When you are careful not to harm anyone through your thoughts, your feelings, your words, you are making room for the Lord to come and dwell within you. This love of self is divine, and that is how we should love ourselves. Those who don't know how to love themselves correctly, can have no love for God or for others. The love of God begins with the love of self, for love must first pass through you, and then rejoin the other Self, above. You must wish to remain pure and shining to please the higher part of yourself which is watching over you. That is how to love oneself, keeping everything intact within.

It is normal to love oneself, Nature has given all her children the instinct to love themselves. Only they need to learn how to love, how to maintain a great respect for order and harmony, how to be conscious of their dignity, of their divinity. Most people understand love of self as the gratification of all their desires in the search for pleasure, whereas in reality, it should be thought of as intelligence, as purity, as sacrifice. Our happiness and our blossoming out depend on an intelligent comprehension of love. The human experience of love leaves the subject far from clear for them. When a man loves a woman for instance, instead of understanding that it is something divine, that it will enable them to accomplish something extraordinary and marvellous, he only seeks one thing: immediate satisfaction for his desire, which ruins everything. Why could he not have waited and benefited from this attraction, this love? If you love someone, don't show it, don't say anything, content yourself with blessing and thanking Heaven for giving you this love. Yes, it is a gift of wonderful conditions enabling you to rise, to have the courage and drive and inspiration that will enable you to carry off great victories. Don't destroy these conditions by wanting to kiss this woman or sleep with her, for afterwards it is all over, there will be complications, endless difficulties and arguments: "You said this to me ... you did that..." And it's finished, all the joy and happiness and inspiration are gone.

It is a blessing to love, that is why you should protect your loving as long as possible, because the day you release it, you turn the page onto upheaval and catastrophe. Love is God Himself, it brings you everything: joy, happiness, inspiration, treasures, and life itself. Why be in such a hurry to spoil it by releasing it, getting rid of it instead of finding more life through it, the eternal life, the divine life? Night and day you can live with love, on the condition of having relationships, of making exchanges with the most sublime creatures in the most glorious regions, and not wasting it on the prosaic and vulgar, so that there is nothing left of you but a pile of ashes. Therefore, love yourself, but your divine Self, and do everything for that Self. No sacrifice should seem too difficult when it is a question of winning over the beloved, to hold her in one's arms and listen to all Nature sing!

Our success, our happiness, depend on the centre, the point that we call God. You see, here is a pen, on which I have had engraved the symbol of the knowledge of the Initiates: a circle with a point in the centre. How should we interpret it? You have seen a schoolroom when the schoolmaster is absent, the schoolboys kick up a racket, they yell and scream and play games and fight . . . it's normal, the teacher isn't there, so it's time to play. But as soon as he arrives, quick! the students rush to their places in silence. In the army, if the general is missing, the soldiers run around in every direction, it is a rout and a stampede, they will retreat and the battle will be lost. But when the general returns, everyone is there to carry out his orders, to carry off the victory!

I could give you many other examples, but the essential thing is for you to understand that the same laws operate within us. The Lord is the head, the chief, the centre, and when He is not there, you know what they say . . . When the cat's away the mice will play . . . and eat up the cheese! When someone says: "I have no need for the Lord, I can get along without Him", I can answer that in effect he will be able to get along, but inside, all the rats and mice will play because the head is missing. The head, the Lord, brings order into our cells. When He is there, they all work in harmony, in peace, and life can circulate freely. If the head is missing, man will get along for a while going about his business, but inside, it turns into a shambles and eventually breaks down. Humans have not understood why it is important to place the Lord at the centre of themselves and so I tell you: if you wish to have order and harmony within you, look for the head, the centre of the circle, because that point, that centre, organizes everything. There is no greater truth than that.

We should love God for ourselves, not for Him. He has no need of us, He is so rich! You have all probably seen the film:

"God Needs Men". Yes, of course, there is some truth in it, but you know, God can get along without them. What can we add that He needs? Our pride? Our vanity? Our wickedness? Our mediocrity? Those are certainly very helpful to the Lord! Actually, it is we who have need of Him. They say it is a proof of intelligence and higher evolution to get rid of the Lord . . . All right, but these people who are so highly intelligent and evolved, why are they always so dissatisfied, so ill and unbalanced? Because they have driven away the head. If you study the Kabbalah, you will see that everything is based on the venerable Head of God, His hair white as snow, His beard, His ears . . . The entire Kabbalah starts with the venerable Head of God, and yet now we are asked to follow the lead of some little idiot who advises us to eliminate this Head!

Understand me once and for all: I am speaking from experience, for me it is not mere theory, all my life has been based on this symbol of the circle with its central point. This centre which is in us, we must find; it is there, somewhere, but not in the centre, and we must find it and place it in the centre. There isn't a creature in existence who doesn't have this centre, but it is floating around somewhere on the periphery along with things that are not so important, and at the centre we have placed our job, or friend, or affair, or car . . . You should start by looking for the Lord, and then place Him in the centre of your life, because from then on, everything will improve for you, your health, your understanding, everything, and the others will begin to love you, because they will feel in you a spring, a centre that is alive and overflowing. If you are not a well-spring, if nothing flows forth from you, how can you expect to be loved? People don't love a grave, or a pit, or an abyss; people love something that is full of life.

Now go ahead on this bright and shining path, with tremendous faith, for it will lead you to the whole of Initiatic science, to everything that is written in the Sacred Books. The years will pass and the events of life will prove to you the truth of what I am saying. One cannot love God unless one loves oneself, because love must pass through the higher part of ourselves in order to escape toward God. Yes, it is all mapped out. When you wish to send messages by radio, you go to the office reserved for that purpose and your message is transmitted, you don't think of crying out into the air so as to be heard at a distance of hundreds and thousands of kilometres ... you need the transmitting apparatus. And we, too, have inside of ourselves all the necessary transmitting equipment: our higher Self, the Universal Soul which lives within us ... For women it is a masculine principle, for men a feminine principle. As long as the message has not been transmitted to the other pole, it cannot be received. When Initiates or mystics pray, they forget themselves to such an extent that it is no longer they who pray, but their spirit, their soul, which transmits the prayer, and the prayer is received in Heaven. As long as your prayer is not sufficiently intense to be transmitted by the other extreme of your being, your spirit, it will never be answered. And whether you call this other extreme, this other pole, Christ, or spirit, or your soul, or your beloved, it is of no importance whatsoever.

It is said in the science of the Initiates that we can find nothing externally that we have not first found internally, because that which you find on the outside, you will not recognize if you have not already seen it inside, you will pass by without seeing it. The more you discover beauty within, the more you discover it outside on the physical plane. Perhaps you think you didn't see it before because it wasn't there ... It was, but you couldn't see it, because inside you there was something not yet developed enough to notice it. Now that you have seen it from within, you will also be able to see it on the outside, because the outside world is made of reflections of the inside world. Never look for anything on the outside that you have not already made the effort to find on the inside.

Once you have found your higher Self, your twin-soul, during your meditation and contemplation, you will keep finding it everywhere in the world, in people's faces, in lakes and mountains and plants and birds, and you will be able to hear its voice. This is the most important truth for those who love each other, otherwise their marriage, their relationship, will be a disaster. If a man has found within himself the feminine principle, and a woman has found the masculine principle, and they wish to work for that principle, to serve it, then let them love each other, let them marry, for their love will be a source of many blessings! This is why I say that the woman should look for the Heavenly Father in her husband, who is God's representative on earth, and the husband should see in his beloved wife the Divine Mother, whom he should love, contemplate and serve. Whereupon, all the treasures of Heaven will be available to them and they will live night and day in beauty, ecstasy and rapture. If not, they will be disappointed, they will suffer, they will begin to speak with disgust against all men and all women ... Simply because that which they knew was not the other's soul or spirit, it was their worn clothing, unhealthy rags. This is what happens to those who haven't been willing to learn the truth, who have refused to listen to the Initiates, who don't wish to know anything: they are betrayed by themselves. It is himself that man punishes when he refuses to be enlightened with the bright light that will open his eyes and show him the way.

The Sacred Books are open before you tonight with all their hidden meaning ... Why hesitate? Go ahead, let nothing stop you, and may God be always with you!

Videlinata, Switzerland, April 8, 1962

Chapter II

Taking the Bull by the Horns – The Caduceus of Mercury

I

Treatises on the subject of alchemy state that in order to obtain the philosophic stone, symbolized by Mercury, the work must be started at the same moment that the Sun enters into the constellation of Aries, and the Moon into Taurus, because Aries is where the Sun is at its most intense, and the Moon is most intense in Taurus. The sign that follows after, Gemini, is the house of Mercury. Thus, you see: Aries (the Sun), Taurus (the Moon) and Gemini (Mercury)... These three signs follow each other, showing that from the union of the Sun and the Moon comes the child, Mercury. The same group, the Sun, Moon and Mercury are together elsewhere in the Zodiac, but today we will just take the three most significant signs: Aries, Taurus and Gemini.

The symbol of Mercury is formed by the solar disc, over which is the crescent of the moon, and to symbolize their union, the sign "+", symbol of addition. The symbol of Mercury (☿) illustrates the union of the Sun and the Moon.

The Sun and the Moon give birth to a child, Mercury, the philosopher's stone. But the philosopher's stone that the alchemists sought is actually a symbol of the transformation of man. They worked with the Sun and the Moon, that is with the two principles, the imagination and the will, and thanks to the work of these two principles, they were able to transform their own matter and become, symbolically, like the Sun and the Moon, radiant and pure. It is not by chance that Aries is the house of Mars, that Taurus is the house of Venus... By working with the

Sun and the Moon, in other words with the two principles, masculine and feminine, by sublimating the sexual force (Venus) and the active, dynamic force of the will (Mars), the alchemist can obtain all the spiritual powers symbolized by Mercury, the magic agent. The Templars represented this magic agent as Baphomet, the monstrous figure that brought accusations of Devil-worship on them. There have been others who called the magic agent Azot, formed by the letters: A, the first letter of the three alphabets: in Latin, A; in Greek, alpha; and in Hebrew, aleph; and the last letter of the three alphabets: Z in Latin; O in Greek; and T in Hebrew. The word signifies that the magic agent was Alpha and Omega, the beginning and the end.

To obtain the magic agent, the alchemists went to enormous trouble, frequently without succeeding, because they didn't know that the work of the will and the imagination must be done not only on the physical plane but also on the spiritual plane. This work is symbolized by the expression: "Take the bull by the horns." Taking the bull by the horns is what the disciple should do to begin the inner work that will bring under control whatever within him that is vulgar, rebellious and violent. Unfortunately these days humans don't take the bull by the horns, they give it complete freedom to trample on everything. You will see how destructive the bull is, especially where young people are concerned.

Taking the bull by the horns represents the work of the will on our imagination, which is connected with sensuality and voluptuousness. Those who have an unbridled imagination have a tendency to be lazy and sensual. The Moon and Venus always go together. But if the Sun steps in with its light and directs the forces in the right direction, the Moon can become extraordinarily useful because of its power to materialize things. I have told you about the different periods that the earth has gone through, the age of Saturn, the age of the Sun, the age of the Moon, for instance, and I explained that the age of the Sun was a time of growth and blossoming, whereas the age of the Moon, on the contrary, was a time of materialization, of concretization. The Sun and the Moon are also symbols of the two processes called in alchemy: "Solve et Coagula": to dissolve and to solidify, to spiritualize and to materialize.

In the symbol of Mercury, the Sun is represented by a circle, and the Moon by a part of a circle, a portion of the sun, which explains the saying in Genesis that God took Eve from one of Adam's ribs. And to show that the combination, this conscious mingling of the two principles, produced Mercury, the Initiates represented Mercury as the Sun and Moon united by the symbol of the earth, which is also the symbol of addition. The profound science of the Initiates is demonstrated by the sign of Mercury. One of its many variations is the Caduceus of Mercury which is still used as an insignia in the world of medicine.

Today, the same symbol is used by scientists in the form of a laser.

The Caduceus of Mercury

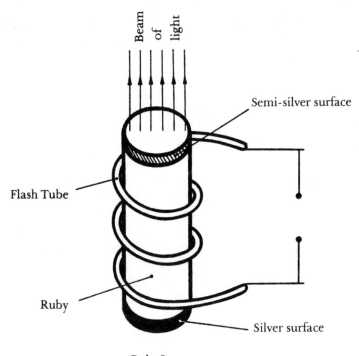

Ruby Laser

A ruby crystal is surrounded by a flash tube which will furnish the necessary energy to produce the "laser effect". When it is working, an intensely strong beam of red light comes out of one end.

This beam represents Mercury, born of the two principles. But the question now is to find the laser inside oneself, it is within ourselves that the "laser" will produce its most formidable results.

Since remotest antiquity, the Initiates have realized within themselves all those things that official science has now discovered: the radio, the telephone, television. Scientists are bringing to the physical plane the laws that exist in the spiritual world. Everything must be realized in matter, this is why all scientists are past Initiates, alchemists, mages and kabbalists, come to realize in matter everything that has already been realized on a spiritual plane. Without the spiritual plane, there would be no way of discovering anything whatsoever on the physical plane. Everything that is below is like that which is above: all that is above in the psychic plane must be materialized below on the physical plane.

In creating the symbol of Mercury, the Initiates wished to teach future generations how to work on the sexual force through the will and the imagination, in order to obtain magic power. The "most forceful force of all forces" of which Hermes Trismegistus speaks, is love. Only love gives life, and nothing is above life; it is the origin of everything. God gave us this force of love so that we would learn to sublimate it by living intensely, so as to have magic powers, so as to be omnipotent. As I said, the symbol of Mercury is the combination of the Sun, the Moon, and the Earth. But if we remove the Moon, that which remains is the symbol of Venus, love. The symbol of Mercury is also the magic wand of the god Hermes, the caduceus, the symbol of the powers he possessed in all regions.

In the sign of Mercury, the Moon which represents the imagination, is there as a receptacle full of water, because the Moon, the feminine principle, is closely connected to water. Below her is the Sun, or fire, which lights the imagination, and still further below is the Earth, the symbol of realization on the physical plane. When an Initiate understands this symbol, he is able to create, to help others, to enlighten, vivify and protect them, for he is omnipotent. If he is given the right conditions, he can turn the earth upside down, because he has understood the essential: the work of the will on the imagination. Just as woman is able to condense life into her breast, the Moon has the power to concretize, to materialize things, to transform them into earth, that is, to realize them on the physical plane. You see, to make the symbols speak, you must take them by the throat and say: "Your purse or your life!" and then they will reveal their secrets. You have to wring it out of them!

The disciple has to defeat the bull, which means he has to dominate this brute force, the savage force of sensuality, and absorb its strength. To overcome the bull doesn't mean to kill it; if you do, there will be no more strength for you to draw on. You must take the bull by the horns, and master the Moon, the imagination which is inseparable from sensuality, except for those who have taken their bull by the horns already, the philosophers and artists and Initiates who have given another direction to their imagination, who make creations and discoveries that enlighten the rest of the world. Those who don't succeed in taking the bull by the horns are allowing their imaginations to gallop around everywhere, exactly like a prostitute who sleeps with anyone and everyone, and then brings monsters and gargoyles into the world. We must always make sure our imaginations have a determined job to do, so that they will produce only the best, the brightest and the most beautiful ideas. A disciple mustn't allow his wife to wander about and sleep with anyone else, he must keep her to himself. Yes, my dear brothers and sisters, our imagination is our wife, she brings our children into the world.

If we look for an interpretation of the caduceus of Mercury, we will find that it is a résumé of the human being. The intertwined serpents curled around the staff represent the two currents that descend from the brain. Starting from the right and left hemispheres, they cross at the nape of the neck, pass through the left and right lungs, cross each other in the solar plexus, pass by the liver and the spleen, cross at the navel, pass by the kidneys, cross each other in the Hara centre, and finally pass through the sexual glands of the man or the ovaries of the woman.

The staff stands for the spinal column. The Initiates of India claim that the force Kundalini slumbers at the base, waiting to be awakened. Starting at the Mouladara chakra, the force Kundalini courses through the central canal of the spinal column called Sushumna. Propelled upwards by breathing and by Ida and Pingala, the two currents on either side of Sushumna, Kundalini rises all the way to the top, the lotus of a thousand petals called the Sahasrara chakra.

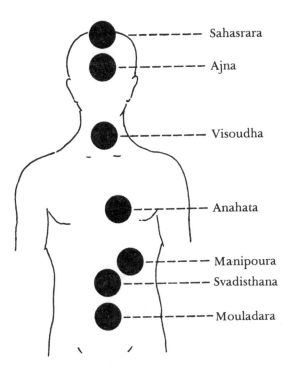

Sahasrara

Ajna

Visoudha

Anahata

Manipoura

Svadisthana

Mouladara

Initiates and yogis who are able to work with the Sun (the positive current of Pingala) and the Moon (the negative current of Ida) awaken the force Kundalini, and make it rise to the top. Once again it is the phenomenon of the laser. The human being is a living laser. To obtain the greatest force of all forces, the magic agent of the universe, we must be able to set the laser in motion.

Remember therefore that you must learn to work with the Moon, the imagination, whilst keeping it pure. The Moon, in its true spiritual sense, is linked with the purity of the imagination. You must also work with light, with the fire of the Sun, with the impartial love of Venus, and finally with the justice of the cross, the Earth, in order to obtain the perfect results you seek. Mercury is the symbol of the perfect human being, whose two currents circulate so harmoniously, so evenly, that he swims in peace, and becomes a radiant centre able to draw all creatures up towards the good.

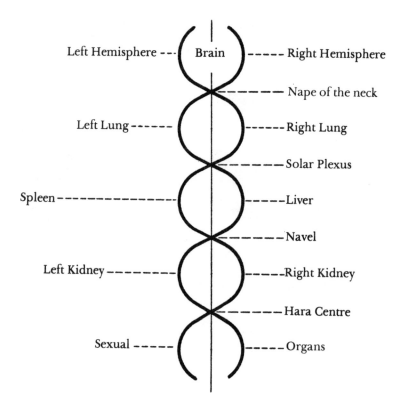

When the Moon is not under the control of Mars and the Sun, it makes humans indolent and inactive; they want to dispense with all effort and rely on machines and devices to do their work. The symbol of Mercury teaches us the contrary, that activity and effort are absolutely indispensable. There is nothing wrong in having machines and devices on the condition that they free man from material tasks so that he can devote himself to a new activity, the spiritual work that he does with his will and imagination, the work of divine creation. Unfortunately, for the moment, that is not the goal towards which men work. They prefer to eliminate the Sun and Mars, all activity and effort, and remain under the influence of the Moon and Venus. They don't realize that this is the best way of becoming degenerate.

I feel as though I have not said anything to you yet, but actually I have said it all. Before you lies Heaven, you have been given to drink, and an ocean lies before you. If you remain the same as before, it means that you have received as much as you are prepared to receive at your stage of evolution, no more. That's what is sad. But by basking in this atmosphere, this love, this harmony, this light and knowledge, you must evolve, and one day you will be able to undertake the most extraordinary things. Even if you don't understand, continue, for nevertheless there will always be something of value, something shining that will be imprinted on your soul.

Sèvres, December 27, 1970

II

There are very few people who know how to work, and what to work on, when it comes to the spiritual, the psychic or inner life. Everyone is busy giving humans all kinds of facts so that they can take up almost any trade or profession on earth, they are forever in school, forever apprentices . . . but inside themselves they remain weak and powerless, and at the slightest sign of trouble or difficulty, they fall flat on their faces.

I know that all the Eastern methods have been introduced to the Western world: yoga, Zen, etc., and people throw themselves into these practices because they feel that they should do something with their wills. They want to learn concentration and meditation; they want to acquire psychic powers. I have nothing against all this, it can even bring good results sometimes, but for the majority, I have my doubts, because these are ancient methods that were good in the past and they were meant for Orientals. For the West, we need other methods more adapted to that mentality, to that way of life, and these are precisely the methods of the Teaching of the Great Universal White Brotherhood. People who throw themselves into Oriental practices without a guide are taking a great risk. Orientals are never without guidance. They have a Master who supervises what they do, the way doctors here have patients under treatment who need observation, in order to make adjustments if they are needed. People who do these things on their own with insufficient knowledge and training endanger their health. More and more now, humans will realize that they should explore the inner world, but they should be wary of the methods available, many of which are dangerous.

The Initiatic work with the Sun and the Moon, with the will and the imagination, is valid for eternity, because the will and the imagination are two fundamental principles in man. This is why the books on alchemy are full of pictures of the Sun and the Moon, the king and queen . . . Nothing exists beyond that: the Sun and the Moon, the male and the female who produce the royal child: the philosophic stone, the elixir of immortal life, the universal panacea, the magic wand, the caduceus of Mercury . . .

Man's mission is to realize Heaven on earth, to resemble his Heavenly Father, the Creator. This glorious mission cannot be accomplished all at once, and he must learn to acquire that which is indispensable for this work: the two principles, active and passive, emissive and receptive, masculine and feminine, the Sun and the Moon, the will and the imagination. The Moon must become imbued with the Sun's brilliance and greatness, and then reflect and propagate that brilliance and greatness.

The Moon is open to every influence, anyone can manifest through her, she has no choice, like water which takes the form of the container into which it is poured. Water, the Moon, and the imagination are all very much the same. If the Sun doesn't take care to influence the Moon (the imagination) it will reflect Hell just as easily. The Initiate makes sure that the Moon, his imagination, his "wife", is not free to wander about, and thanks to the Sun, she receives both light and eternity. Then the Moon becomes an extraordinary and adorable wife, and other divine laws are there to realize on the physical plane that which is formed by the imagination. That is the meaning of the cross at the base of the sign of Mercury. The cross is the cubic stone which signifies the earth. For the alchemists, the cubic stone was the virgin ground on which they were to build the edifice.

Each day the disciple should be making grandiose and noble plans in his mind so as to realize them on earth. First of all, he must work with his imagination, and then put his will and his heart to work to accomplish that which he has imagined. It is not enough to dream of fine projects and then do nothing about them. The disciple's projects must be reflected in his behaviour and in his actions on the physical plane, so that the whole world can see that he created something above and brought it down to take root on earth.

Whether the spirit works on our soul or the will on the imagination, whether the Sun fertilizes the Moon or man fertilizes woman, the result will always be the creation of a child. And what is that child? When you put a pot of water on the fire, (here the pot is the Moon!), the water changes into steam. The forceful force of all forces is this steam, this vaporized water. Because of the will working on the imagination, because of the spirit working on the soul, the Sun on the Moon, the man on the woman, there is a force born which is the child, Mercury, who has every possibility of carrying out fantastic projects. Separately, the Sun and Moon cannot achieve much. Once separated, the fire burns everything and the water floods everything. When they are united, they produce a force, the philosophic stone which has the power to transform any metal into gold. In the "Emerald Table" it says of this force: "The Sun is its father, the Moon its mother, it was carried in the womb (of the Moon) by the wind, and the earth is its nurse." The earth is the cross, the cubic stone.

The Bible says: "Increase and multiply". Humans have applied this commandment only on the physical plane where it creates a lot of complications: there is now no more room or food, and men are obliged to kill each other, so the commandment ends up being harmful. It is not that I wish to correct or change it, but I say that it is no longer valid for this era, that it was valid only for a certain epoch. Humans have perpetuated this commandment, and now the results are no longer good. The effects are bad for mankind. It must be understood in the symbolic sense where it will always be valid.

The disciple should think about the work he must do with his will on his imagination, and this work concerns men and women. He should fertilize his own wife on the spiritual plane, and create children there, thousands of angelic children to go off into space and work for him. You know how the story always ends: "And they lived happily ever after and had many children". Have many children, yes, but not only on the physical plane. What is an Initiate? He is the father of a family who has many children around him, hanging onto his coat and digging into his pockets, but they love him, they have so much love for him that he is never disturbed, they are never a nuisance. When he needs to, he calls his children to him and says: "Here, go and take these gifts to so and so ... And you, go and pull that one's ear ..." and they obey. They are the children of his own flesh and blood. An ordinary man is a lonely man without children. There is nobody to help him. Most of you don't know this, but it is a fact, known and lived by Initiates.

At Christmas I spoke to you about the birth of the Christ-child. The Christ-child is Mercury. We all know that Jesus was born in Palestine two thousand years ago, but the idea behind this event must be understood, it has cosmic dimensions, it is of universal importance. This birth must also take place within every one of us. The Christ-child is the force that sleeps within us which we must bring to life.

Before coming down on earth, man works on his physical body, and as I explained before, the physical body is the caduceus of Mercury with the currents coming down on either side of the body, starting in the brain and crossing each other at the level of the organs. Man is the product of the work of the will and the imagination, of the spirit and the soul, materialized on the physical plane. He is the caduceus of Mercury and he can create in the three worlds. At the moment he is only creating on the physical plane, and he must learn how to create in the other worlds.

The Caduceus of Mercury is the most forceful force of all forces, it is life in its highest degree of manifestation. When man develops in himself the caduceus of Mercury, this life force will circulate in all creatures throughout the universe and rise as high as the stars. It is a superior degree of life, the true force, life that bursts forth with something beyond vitality. Vitality is the bull . . . all men have life, that's certain, but in most men it manifests itself as a destructive force. When they have too much vitality, people can no longer dominate themselves, they use it to devour, to violate and to assassinate others. Vitality must be directed, it must be intensified and spiritualized so as to be transformed into life that is divine.

That is why you should be trying day and night to spiritualize your life, to send it out into the universe, to bring new life and light to all creatures. This is the idea behind the ancient symbol of Mercury, shown with wings on his feet. The feet have certain very important centres, and if you can develop them, you will be able to move about in space spiritually, and even physically.

The caduceus of Mercury is life, sublime life. When you radiate this life, you will have extraordinary power. If your life reaches no further than a few centimetres away from your body, you are weak and puny and unable to do anything. But if your radiance extends several miles, then you can have power over all creatures. The more intense and far reaching your emanations, the more power you have.

I am explaining the importance of this work so that you will take it seriously and leave a lot of other useless occupations behind, for they can bring you nothing but suffering. Work on yourselves, keep working on yourselves, until the greatest force of all forces begins to show in you.

Sèvres, January 3, 1971

Chapter III

The Serpent – Isis Unveiled

The Maître reads from the Meditations of the Master Peter Deunov:

"There is a legend of Buddha falling in love with a beautiful young girl. In her he saw the divine principle. But one day when he was looking at her he became so enchanted with her beauty that he fell asleep. As she had work to do, the beautiful young girl went away: in other words, the divine principle abandoned her, and there remained only her human astral nature which wound around him like a snake and wouldn't let go. Buddha was full of great learning and wisdom and he knew the only way he could free himself was by being humble, by having the ability to diminish himself. Up until then, he had known how to grow in wisdom and increase in size, but to free himself from the serpent he was forced to learn to reduce himself or die. Little by little he shrank, getting smaller and smaller until there was almost nothing left of him and thus he extricated himself from the serpent's hold."

The serpent is still worshipped in certain regions of India. It is a whole religion with its priests and priestesses, and the serpent has his servants as though he were a divinity . . . On certain days sacrifices are made; the priestess annoints herself with oil and the powder of a special stone, and then she dances before the serpent. The snake lifts his head erect and an extraordinary contest begins between the woman and the snake until she is able to enchant him. Finally, it's fantastic, they seem to want to embrace. Many priestesses have died that way, bitten by the serpent during this rite, but the tradition continues.

All the people of the world have almost the same symbol of the serpent or the dragon. In Europe there are stories of the dragon who captures the beautiful princess, innocent and pure, whom he imprisons in a castle. The poor princess languishes in prison praying tearfully for a knight to deliver her. One after the other all the knights present themselves and are consumed by the dragon, who hoards their treasures in the subterranean passages of the castle. Finally one day a young knight appears, a prince, handsomer and purer than the others, to whom a sorceress has revealed the secret of conquering the dragon, revealing the dragon's weakness, and the precise moment when he is vulnerable and can be wounded and bound hand and foot. So this privileged prince, well armed and well disciplined, carries off the victory and frees the princess. Whereupon what kisses they exchange! The treasures that have accumulated in the castle over the centuries all belong to the handsome prince who was able to triumph over the dragon because of his knowledge and because of his extraordinary purity. Together, mounted on the dragon, they travel all over the world.

In the story told by the Master, Buddha nearly succumbed because in reality this serpent is not found outside man, but within man, where it is the symbol of the sexual force which we carry within us and against which we must wrestle. The dragon, or the serpent, is sexual force; the castle is the physical or the astral body of man; the princess is the soul which the knight, the disciple's ego, must liberate. The arms he uses to fight the dragon, the sword, etc. are the means at his disposal, his will, and the knowledge of how to conquer this force and use it. The dragon becomes the servant of the disciple; he serves as his horse, his mount to carry him through space. Now you can see the clarity and simplicity of the eternal language of symbols.

We find another version of this adventure in the story of Theseus who, with the help of the thread given him by Ariadne, is able to find his way through the labyrinth and kill the Minotaur. The Minotaur is another symbol of sexual force, the powerful and prolific bull which is our inferior nature, and which we must harness and put to work on the land, like an ox. The labyrinth signifies the castle, the physical body, and Ariadne signifies the higher soul which leads man to victory.

The serpent is an inexhaustible theme. But the reptile that we know as the snake is only a pale reflection of another force which exists in Nature. In ancient astrology the Zodiac is shown as a serpent on which are placed the twelve signs corresponding to each part of the human body, beginning with the head, Aries, and finishing with the tail, Pisces.

What is interesting about the story I just read to you, is that it concerns Buddha, this wonderful Master whom we find also had to wrestle with the serpent. If Buddha himself was not spared, how much less all the others! All the Initiates must pass through this test. The young girl he loves has a dual nature, divine and human (or astral); like all women, she possesses the two natures and manifests one or the other as the case may be. It says that Buddha loved the divine principle in this girl. Yes, and as long as he could resist the physical attraction her beauty had for him, he remained in the impersonal region where there was neither desire nor lust but only wonderment, and he was in no danger. But Buddha, without meaning to, captivated by the young girl's charm, allowed his inferior nature to be awakened and he "went to sleep". Because when the inferior nature awakes in man, the other nature falls asleep, he forgets his good and wise resolutions, and he obeys the advice of his inferior nature. Afterwards he is astonished that he forgot the promises he made with so much sincerity.

When Buddha fell asleep, the young girl left him for her other work. This means that the divine principle was eclipsed and as it was no longer there to protect Buddha with light, the serpent wrapped him in his coils. Buddha fought, but despite all his knowledge and learning he was unable to extract himself. Finally he understood that he was not the one to conquer, that his limited nature would never be able to win, and instead of facing the formidable cosmic force which has been stored for generation after generation in the subconscious, instead of wrestling and fighting alone, he diminished himself, he humbled himself and gave every chance to the divine principle within to manifest. It was the divine power which won, while he himself, his personality, was so small that he was able to escape. What does this mean? I will give you an example to enable you to understand.

Suppose a disciple has been able to win several victories. He has met some pretty girls and not allowed himself to be tempted, and he is proud of himself; he thinks: "I'm strong, I have conquered temptation." That is when he is in danger, because at that moment traps are being set for him of such subtlety that he will have to succumb, there is no doubt, because he is not humble . . . He's proud and counts on himself, deluded by his little victories. He doesn't yet know the cleverness of the serpent. It says in Genesis: "The serpent was more subtle than any beast of the field which the Lord God had made." It is when man is surest of himself that the serpent surprises him. A true disciple knows this, he is fearful after carrying off a few victories, and he thinks: "What next? I shouldn't be able to win, it's too soon for me to win!" Not only does he remain vigilant but he knows that it will do no good to wrestle with the problem by himself and he begs the Lord to come and give him His aid. You notice that in story books it never says that the Knight is able to win alone; others are always there to give him advice, or secrets, or arms.

The most interesting point in this story is that Buddha managed to overcome the serpent's hold not by force but by humility. Because as long as he is dealing with human forces the serpent will always win, his roots are profoundly sunk deep in Nature. You must understand that if you have failed heretofore in your fight against the serpent, it is because you are fighting alone, making yourself larger when you should be diminishing

yourself. It is such an important point, but very few people know
it. No one ever thinks of shrinking, of growing smaller, only some
little insects have understood that they can fool the enemy and
escape by pretending to be dead. Of course, it doesn't always work
because everybody knows they're pretending and are not really
dead . . .

Let us come back to the other interesting part of the story, in
which it says that Buddha loved the divine principle in this young
girl. How many times have I repeated: Men and women should
see each other as bearers of the divine principle, because then
they run no danger, they have wings, they surpass themselves and
discover the world, they are creators. Seen this way, everything
changes. We must know how to see creation as a means of going
as far as the Creator, it is a ladder, Jacob's Ladder if you will, and
each thing, each being, represents a degree, a step up in order to
reach all the way to the Lord.

If all Nature presents you with an indescribable treasure:
stones, flowers, trees, butterflies, birds, fish, and if through them
you can understand the Creator's plans, why is the question of
men and women so complicated? Look at the advice given by
generations of Christians, to flee all women, to avoid looking at
them and above all, never to see them naked even if only to
admire them. Of course if these rules even exist, it is because of
the weakness of men, and that is the whole question: people's
degree of evolution. For someone who is highly evolved, whether
a woman is dressed or not makes no difference, he will always be
tranquil and he will always see God everywhere.

The Mysteries say that the Initiate must be able to contemplate
Isis unveiled. Because he is pure and wise, the Initiate knows how
to contemplate Isis, the Divine Mother, Mother Nature, who is
manifest everywhere. It is Isis herself who wishes him to have the
joy of knowing all her secrets, to behold her at last in all her
beauty and purity and brilliance. Symbolically, idealistically, a
woman who is naked before her beloved, is the same as Isis

unveiled before the eyes of the Initiate. But people haven't understood this. They do nothing all their lives but repeat the mysteries of Initiation, the mysteries of Isis, but without realizing it. Why is it the custom to wrap the bride in a veil which she is supposed to remove on her wedding night, for her beloved to behold her? Almost no one knows the real reasons for such customs and all dwell on the lower, most vulgar and material side, instead of preparing themselves to understand one of the greatest mysteries. They are not prepared, and that is why there are so many abnormalities later. The young married couple go on a "honeymoon", and it is their understanding that the honeymoon is a period during which they can indulge in sexual pleasure to the point of nausea. That is how they enact the eternal symbol: the Initiate presented to Isis, his betrothed.

There are also the Nuptials of the Lamb that come from the same Initiatic mysteries, only on a higher level of knowledge, and has nothing to do with the nuptials they practice now, in which people find neither joy, peace, liberation, knowledge, or enlightenment of any kind; on the contrary, the reverse occurs and they lose their peace. If people go on seeing things in this erroneous way, they mustn't hope to find what they are seeking! A mother is asked: "Where is your daughter? – She's gone to Venice with her husband on their honeymoon." There, the honeymoon! And what are they doing, those two idiots who have no knowledge whatsoever? Overindulging in pleasure until they are both disgusted. As they are blind, neither will see the beauty of the other, nor their spirit and soul, nor all the splendour they have inside, they will see only skin, legs, and the physical, that's all. Poor humanity! The Initiate doesn't think about going on binges, he is too busy preparing himself for the wedding feast of the Lamb, for his betrothed, for ecstasies beyond belief.

When these truths are understood all the rest seems pale. All the wrong ideas that fill the heads of the religious will be swept away by the powerful light of knowledge. Finally, humanity will be able to breathe the purer air, and taste the joy of the Nuptials of the Lamb. All are predestined to live this joy. You will say: "Even the old?" Of course, they are more prepared to live with a bridegroom than the young are, for their love is a different kind of love, their thoughts and their ideals are more elevated. They are more prepared to taste the joys of divine love.

When men have learned how to contemplate the divine principle in woman, whether she is naked or clothed, they will no longer want to throw themselves on her, no longer will they lose their heads. Instead they will say: "O Divine Mother, how beautiful you are! I understand why the entire world seeks you and needs you, you are the source of life!"

You are all aware of the power of the two principles. What woman can deny having seen the face of a man, in the street or in a train, in a film or book, that completely upset her? And what man has never been upset at the sight of a young girl's face? It is clear, there is no doubt that the two principles are powerful, active, and that they influence one another, with the goal of creating. No one can deny it. But what is not known, is the measure, the proportions, the distances, the way of looking at things so as to create harmonious states, divine conditions, instead of always being disturbed and in pieces, full of regrets. Who can deny that the feminine principle and masculine principle are both extremely powerful? The entire world is in motion thanks to the energy that the two principles emanate when they are with each other – they are exalted and this exaltation is the power of the laser I mentioned earlier.

The Initiates have always known and made use of these two powers, and it is thanks to their knowledge that they were able to create batteries enabling them in order to do what they wished to do. These batteries were men and women united together consciously and harmoniously. Men and women have no idea yet what tremendous forces Nature has given them. Put to good use, these forces are able to produce phenomena of cosmic importance. But to do that, one needs to be pure and full of wisdom and light, otherwise there will be nothing but catastrophe.

Wisely, carefully, we are going to work to clear the way, to enlarge consciousness, and to spread further than ever before the idea of purity. People think that a young girl or a young boy are pure because they know nothing yet about relationships between men and women. But if you could see what goes on in the heads and hearts of some of them, you would be aghast to find that they are more vicious and more dissolute than adults. The imagination is more prolific among young people. Some are pure of course, but then they are so ignorant and so vulnerable that anyone can come along and pluck them. Purity that is blind cannot last very long, it involves much more than not kissing or being kissed. First of all we must be enlightened, for everything is purified by light, and without light nothing is pure; and only then should we add feeling. And if enlightenment is there, the feelings will be pure.

Let us return to the subject of nakedness. The Initiates talk about knowing the naked truth. The naked truth is Isis which the Initiates contemplate without her veil. The veils correspond to the seven planes: the physical, the etheric, the astral, the mental, the causal, the buddhic and the atmic planes. When the seventh veil is removed, they contemplate the Divine Mother, Mother Nature, naked, that is to say in its purest and most subtle substance, when it is completely united with the spirit. In life, whoever it is you wish to know, try to know him for himself and not only for his appearance. To know your Master it will not be enough to watch him while he eats and drinks, you will never know him by looking at the outer envelope; but if you remove the outer coverings you will come to the region where he really lives, and there you will know him. He is not Isis, but the veiled

Osiris, and if you take his appearance, one of the veils, for himself, you will quickly grow weary, but if you go on and discover what is behind the veils, you will never tire and you will uncover a source of endless joy.

This is how I look at you. If this were not my way of seeing you, long before this, I would have had enough! I would have said: "But this is not interesting, they're always the same little old faces!" Happily, this is not the way I think. I undressed you long ago, exactly as men do when they meet a woman. But don't misunderstand me, the tendency man has to undress the woman in order to look at her has never been properly understood, it was Nature who gave him this instinct so that he would go further than the outer appearance, beyond and higher, where she is truly naked, in all her splendour and purity and light. Above, there is no shame, she is not contemplated for her physical body but for her soul, her divinity. Humans don't know how to interpret Nature's language, they feel certain instincts and stop at their grossest expressions, they capitulate too easily and it is all over.

So when I say that I undress you, don't misunderstand me. I mean that I don't wish to know you only on the physical plane but elsewhere, on the divine plane and when I look at you, I see that you are sons and daughters of God. It's extraordinary, I live in joy, and life flows. Otherwise I would have picked up my hat and gone off long ago. Should you not behave the same way towards me instead of always looking at the outside? It's alright for a while, but don't stop there forever because you will not gain much. I say this for your good, so that you will find the unending joy that is life. The form is necessary, but it won't be satisfactory for very long, it is only a point of departure, like a flask which is only necessary to contain the perfume, to protect the quintessence which is life.

You should always concentrate on the spirit, which gives life, which spreads light, which vibrates and creates worlds . . . Then you will never be disappointed. Mere form can never satisfy you unless it is animated, alive, and even then it is really the life that quenches our thirst and not the form. When we look at a painting it is the life in the painting that interests us. Yes, life can be found in a painting, the life of its creator, the painter who put something of himself into his painting. You can think of men and women as paintings in which the Creator has put life, His own life, and that is what we should be seeking in each other. If this is not the case, we must expect quarrels, divorce, tragedies of all kinds . . . it is fatal.

Now if you ask why the Initiates so admire beauty in creatures, I will tell you. True Initiates are always looking for the harmony and the perfection which is above, and they know that these qualities are reflected by stones and animals, plants, mountains, lakes, rivers, oceans, stars, everywhere, and they also know that nowhere is this harmony, this beauty, this perfection better demonstrated than in the human body. Everywhere else it is scattered, the oceans are only a part of the cosmic body, rivers are another, the sky and mountains still another. Only men and women reflect the cosmic body in its entirety. God produced the universe in man and woman. That's why, when they see a creature who reflects better than others the splendours of the universe, the Initiates contemplate him with delight in order to be themselves linked to divine beauty. They think: "There is a creature who reflects the virtues of God", and while looking at her, they rediscover divine beauty. Ordinary men and women cannot perceive the divine beauty in humans, they throw themselves on whatever is beautiful and spoil it, like a herd of horses galloping through a field and trampling on the flowers. Initiates are so amazed at beauty, at the splendour of Heaven, that they draw an enormous amount of inspiration, strength, energy, and will power with which to continue their work.

Whilst on this subject I will tell you one other very interesting thing. You know that all the organs of the human body correspond to certain forces that circulate in the cosmos. It is in connection with these forces that the different organs of the physical body are formed. Several years ago, I told some of you the cosmic region to which the breasts of woman belong, and you were surprised. People think their sole purpose is to feed the child, which is only one of their purposes; there are others which people ignore. I told you that the left breast is in relation with the currents of the moon, and the right breast with the Milky Way, and if woman were conscious of this relationship, it would be of enormous help to her in her spiritual evolution. Most of the time she is ignorant of the fact that in this way she is in communication with Nature and humanity. Even whilst ignorant of this fact, this etheric and magnetic communication still takes place. She both receives and gives through the two breasts. A short time after revealing this, I visited a museum in Spain and saw a painting by an unknown painter representing a naked woman with the Moon on her left breast and the Milky Way coming out of her right breast. I was surprised and happy to see this confirmation of the truth. The painter was surely an Initiate.

The human body is a summary of the universe. The disciple must know how to look at it and respect it and marvel at it, and especially to take it as the point of departure to raise himself to the sublime world above, becoming part of it and glorifying the Lord, and thus advancing along the path of evolution. Then he will discover all the secrets of Nature, for Isis, who has no further need to suffer from violations of her body before the disciple, will reveal herself to him. She will say: "This is a human being who cares, who loves, respects and admires me. I will show myself to him." Truth will be revealed, for truth is Isis. Truth is above and not buried below under the veils of illusion, Maya. Truth reveals itself to the one who knows how to treat the mysteries of love correctly.

Le Bonfin, July 24, 1962.

Supplementary notes

Some people have a strange idea of the state of man when he is in Heaven. They think he must be there with only his head and nothing more; his liver, stomach, intestines and above all his sexual organs are not noble enough to go with him. But I tell you that man goes intact to Paradise, and if only you knew how splendid and beautiful and pure he is, just as God created him originally! He has lungs as well, but in another form, he has a brain and ears and eyes, but also in another form, or rather another quintessence, because above there are no more forms, but currents, lights, and forces. His body functions as though he still had a stomach, arms and legs, nothing is missing, they are all there but in the shape of virtues and qualities and faculties. Our physical organs are actually a reflection, a condensation of our qualities and virtues; and if you could see a human being in this state with all the colours and lights that shine forth from him, you would never grow tired of looking.

Official science is still very far from knowing what the human being is, and how he was formed by God in His workshops above. Only clairvoyants and the great Masters have been able to go that far and see, and afterwards reveal that the human being above has no form, that he is made of forces, currents, energies, lights and emanations, which, when condensed, become physical organs as we know them. Thus our stomach, liver, spleen, brain, eyes, ears, legs and arms are forces in the higher world. And when man is unreasonable, his light grows dim, he loses his virtues one by one and the organs corresponding to these virtues begin to weaken. This is the explanation for all our physical disorders and illnesses.

Le Bonfin, August 1, 1975.

Chapter IV

The Power of the Dragon

In the Christian religion, the Devil is likened to a dragon, and
the Devil they say, smells of sulphur. All inflammable products
like petrol, dynamite and fuel mixtures, which produce flames
and dreadful odours, are the dragon. The dragon also exists in
the human being, it is a combustible fire which could carry him
up into space. But if he doesn't know how to use it, instead of
being propelled towards the heights, towards Heaven, he will be
dashed to the ground and swallowed up.

The dragon is in ourselves. There is a dragon for each one of
us but there is also a collective dragon, which Saint John
mentioned in the Apocalypse, saying that it would be bound and
tied for a thousand years and then thrown into the abyss. This
means that humanity's collective force which propels humans
into directions that are far from divine, provoking fighting and
killing, will one day be disciplined and oriented and sublimated.
What else could they do with him in the abyss? Leave him like
that? No, he will be disciplined and tamed, he will have
wonderful teachers who will make him go through an
apprenticeship, and he will be given pedicures and manicures
and dental treatments to make him decent, harmless and
sensible.

The dragon should not be killed, he should be trained . . . or
eaten! You laugh? . . . Read what the Jews tell us in the Talmud,
they say there is a monster living at the bottom of the ocean,
called the Leviathan – a monster that represents evil – and at the
end of the world, he will be caught and cut up in pieces, salted
and put into storage to serve as a sumptuous feast for the
Righteous. Yes, this is what it says! Just look at the feast that is in

store for humans, dear brothers and sisters, but on condition that they find themselves among the Just, of course. I don't know what the others will eat, but we the Righteous (yes, we had better say it ourselves because if we wait for others to say it for us, we may wait a long time) we must prepare ourselves to feast on the flesh of this monster. It will no doubt pose a few problems, for suppose it is tough as shoe leather, and we are toothless, what do we do? Perhaps there will be sauces and all sorts of preparations to make it tender. And a lot depends on which piece you get, there's a whole geography of carving involved. And then of course we could put what is left over in tins . . . What a wonderful prospect! Hundreds of factories all busy putting the Leviathan in tins, for the thousands of people who will be at the feast. Let the Righteous rejoice and rub their hands together, their future is secure!

You see dear brothers and sisters, there are several ways of using evil. You should know that you have within yourselves these formidable energies, these combustibles able to propel you to the heights. As long as you ignore the fact that they are forces you can use, you will be burned, reduced to ashes, or projected into the depths of the earth. From now on think of sexual love as the dragon, as the most formidable force, able to set people in motion. Furthermore it is always this force that sets people in motion, that makes them go to work. It is always love, good or bad, which is the driving power, and not money, as people think. People use money to win the woman they love, or an object they want.

We should learn to use this extraordinary driving force, there are examples from which to learn before us everywhere. What does a cook do when she wants to boil water? She pours water in a pot and places it over the fire, for without the pot, the water will extinguish the fire and evaporate; there must be a screen between the two elements. In planes, cars, boats, the fuel is always placed so that it will not come in contact with the passengers and burn them. In the same way, the disciple must keep his love from burning the heart or the soul of the person he loves. Young girls often have lovely ideas about love, but after their first experience, they are disappointed and disheartened, the poetry has vanished, doubtless because the man used methods he shouldn't have used.

If people lose the marvellous ideas they have in their souls to start with, it is because love has been for them a destructive fire which burned everything it touched, instead of being the force that exalts, that sends them on their way towards Heaven feeling encouraged, invigorated and renewed. Why is it that love always destroys that which is good, when its rôle is, on the contrary, to increase and strengthen the best in us?

The first thing to know is that there are two kinds of love: one that is only sensual, with no tenderness, intelligence or delicacy involved; it is the same hunger that prompts the wild beast to throw himself on his prey and then calmly lick his chops. The fact that the other person has been devoured is unimportant as long as one is satisfied. Whereas with the other kind of love, you try to forget yourself, even if you are starved and thirsty, you think first about the other person, about protecting him, enlightening him and bringing him everything you have that will contribute to his peace and contentment. There is no limit to the development of two people who love each other in this way, their love is like fire from the sun, it brings them life and immortality. The heavens open up for two people who have discovered the meaning of life. They emanate something so subtle and radiant that everyone stops to stare at them as they pass by.

As long as you are in this school of the Great Universal White Brotherhood you should at least learn a better way of loving: I present you the dragon, dear brothers and sisters. He is most powerful, he has tremendous energy. If you can subdue him and tame him, he will carry you throughout the universe.

Sèvres, April 4, 1968.

Chapter V

Spirit and Matter:
The Sexual Organs
I

A new culture is coming, a culture that is both universal and fraternal. Once men have learned to understand and love each other, all mankind will become one family. I don't mean that you will all sleep together in one dormitory, in the same bed, but that men will all work, sing, meditate and pray together; then it will be wonderful to be united.

Nature has given each one of us the instinct to flee solitude as if it were the most terrible weight, which is right if we know the best way of escaping solitude. How many boys and girls have solved this problem? They are unhappy because they would like to have a partner with whom to sing a duet but they don't find him, and so they fade and wilt away. Why did the duet have to be physical? Is there no other way? Yes, there are many ways of avoiding solitude. Why must it always be according to the old traditions? Why must it always mean possessing someone?

Woman especially has the tendency to possess, she must have something of her own, at least a child. She sees that the man is always escaping her, she can't hold him, so she holds on to the child. When he is tiny and needs her protection, she is happy taking care of him. But as soon as he grows up, he leaves her also, and once again, she's miserable, because finally she has nothing to possess at all. Her need to possess makes everything complicated. You say: "And doesn't man also want to possess?" No, all he cares about is enjoyment – to put it baldly – in a physical way. For him, possession is to take advantage and run.

Whereas the woman thinks first of all about getting a firm hold on the man, and only then is she willing to give him the rest. The man says: "Don't worry, afterwards everything will work out, first let's taste this." And the woman who is not stupid knows that once he's tasted, he'll leave, and so she answers: "No, first sign here." And she forces him to make a promise, to commit himself.

Every manifestation of men and women, all the mysteries of their physical, emotional, moral and intellectual lives have their origin in what are called the "private parts." These organs represent a resumé of the man and woman, and each one has this resumé, without knowing that that is where everything can be deciphered, that there, in the organs' geometric structure, in their function, lie the answers to the most philosophic questions. We carry on us all our wealth and all the keys, without noticing that we are rich, that we possess in ourselves the knowledge, the criteria, everything. It's unbelievable!

Thus it is the nature of woman to amass and to hold, whereas man is by nature a spendthrift, a waster. Everyone has noticed this but no one knows why it is so; it's clear but humans have not drawn the parallel. Man's character and woman's character can be explained by the structure of their sexual organs. The woman is possessive, because if she were not, there would be no creation; her role is to take and gather in, to confine and hold, to preserve and conserve.

In Bulgaria we say: "It is because the woman hoards that the house is full." Of course there are also spendthrift women but that is because they are not really women but men in disguise. Cosmic Intelligence had a reason for giving woman the need to attract and to retain for if she didn't there would be no children. If men are wasters, it's not so serious, there will still be enough first matter. A large amount of grain and seed is needed to produce even a small crop. Nature realized that she had to let each man be generous, so there would be at least one birth, otherwise everything would be scattered, or fall on barren soil. But if woman was allowed to be as generous as man, the result would be sterility. That is why she so treasures the little that comes her way.

This physical need to take in and hold onto things, which is the characteristic of woman, is also the cause of her worst fault: jealousy. In the case of kings and sultans, what did their women, their favourites, do? Every woman in the court or harem had one desire: to monopolize the king or sultan, to be the favourite, the first, the best-loved. And to be that, they spared no effort including lies and conspiracies. It was a battle to the end between the women, to possess the sovereign. And why must they possess him? Because it meant certain advantages, the woman who won was flattered that the king's glance fell on her, that she had been chosen, and thus her dearest wish was satisfied. That is why, to triumph over the others, she would stop at nothing. You say: "But that was in the past, among the Turks!" And in France wasn't it the same thing? History is full of examples – The kings of France, Louis XIV, Louis XV . . . how many women wanted to capture them!

It's natural for a woman to want to be decorative, to assert herself, for a man who is worth the trouble. But the terrifying thing with women is that they won't accept that other women should have the same favours and advantages they have. And rather than conquer this fault, they do everything to increase it. Woman can't live without jealousy, it torments them but they can't live without it; it's as though without it they were no longer stimulated, they are bored. Whereas jealousy pushes them into clandestine affairs, and then, life seems interesting!

Women have a tendency to envy in other women whatever makes them more noticed and admired than themselves . . . and what woman will forgive the man who gives a little love and tenderness to another, rather than to her? She will be furious, she will not stop until she has found some way of punishing him. But if you show her love and tenderness, ah, that's different, that's normal, that's only fair, it is her due. When a woman is furious with a man, it is usually because he hasn't given her what she was hoping for, and gave it to someone else instead. When a girl hates a boy, it's because he kisses someone else instead of her. You may say that this is a cruel analysis but you are wrong – it is a correct one. Is a woman unhappy at being loved? That's all she is waiting for, all she wants. And if the man prefers someone else, she will exaggerate and twist whatever the facts are, so that he will be in the wrong, be condemned and perhaps even be killed. That is the reason why women must develop generosity, and learn to rejoice in the happiness of others.

Now we will discuss this question of the man and woman's sexual organs from a more philosophic aspect.

If the invisible world restricts certain people, placing limitations and constraints in their path, it is to awaken in them the wish and the will to conquer, to liberate themselves. With gunpowder, if you shut it up and compress it and put a match to it, everything will explode, but if you give it plenty of space, even if you light it, it will only go fffft! If man lives too easy a life, his existence will amount to exactly the same thing! fffft. But if he is constrained, if he suffers, his spirit will rejoice because he will have to make the effort to break out. Man suffers and is tearful and miserable, but the spirit rejoices. The same thing happens between men and women. Why does the man wish to be held tightly, to be constrained and limited during love? Because there is something within him that rejoices. If the woman gave him unlimited space, he would feel nothing.

These are things you have never thought about and yet you think you know all there is to know in the field of love. For me, it is not the physical manifestations that are interesting, but what lies behind, the philosophic aspect, the divine and profound aspect hidden behind these manifestations. It is the woman who must envelop the man, she encircles him, and he is lost somewhere in space, like the spirit, buried deep in matter. Why does matter always envelop the spirit? Humans have understood nothing at all about that either. The whole philosophy of creation, the relation between spirit and matter, is to be found in these organs that everyone has and which they use night and day without understanding. You must try to understand!

Humans are plunged up to their necks in physical love, night and day, without ever understanding the sublime truths hidden in the act, because they don't take the time, nor have they the wits to understand. They are too deeply submerged in sensations. Whereas those who don't practice these things have time to understand what the others practice. How is it that I have had time to understand the greatest mysteries of Creation?

Le Bonfin, August 8, 1963.

II

Why is it that men and women seek each other out? Because of their physical bodies? No, it is in order to receive something else, something more subtle and more alive, called love. And when they've found it they are happy and satisfied. If it were only the physical body they were looking for, they would be able to cut off a piece and eat or drink it. But since the body remains intact, it must be that they draw on something else through it, some kind of fluid or emanation. You see how little they know, they don't even realize what they are seeking . . . If it is really the physical body, how can they be surfeited while the body remains the same, intact?

Actually, the physical bodies of men and women are only conductors, transmitters of Heaven or of Hell, depending on what they have in their heads or in their hearts at the time. With the same organ they can stir either Heaven or Hell but the organs themselves are not specific. For instance, you take a knife that can wound or kill someone and with the same knife you can set a prisoner free, or operate on a man whose life is in danger. In the same manner, the sexual organs are neither good nor bad, it all depends on you. When you come in contact with someone by touching them, you can either contaminate them or you can save them, it all depends on what you have in your heart and soul. With the same person in your arms, you can reach either Heaven or Hell, you can stir up all the devils which will never leave you alone again, which will beat you up and wear you down, or else you can reach the angels, the heavenly beings. These are things no one ever thinks about, we do everything blindly and automatically. We have a need, so we go ahead without pausing to reflect that behind this act might be a whole science, a prodigious science. Heaven has given us these organs for a specific purpose, they are predestined to carry out fantastic plans but for the moment they are used to do each other harm and to stir up the astral regions.

How many more things there are to be said on this subject! It is a tremendously rich and large and important subject. Important because that is where life comes from. And instead of storing up life we spoil it, waste it. I will let you meditate on this subject, and maybe you will make some discoveries. I mustn't tell you everything, I am not allowed to. These are truths that are so sacred that if they are given to you as though they were unimportant and nothing much, the consequences could be disastrous. If you are not evolved, if you have no high ideal, even the truth can be detrimental. When we get a hold of the truth too easily without sufficient preparation, it becomes an obsession, we can think of nothing else but are unable to do anything about it, and it can be very dangerous.

But I will add a few words which may be useful to you. One day, a young girl came to see me about a problem that was worrying her. She was most unhappy because everywhere she looked, in all things, she saw the image of the male sexual organ, and the more she fought against this image, the more she became obsessed by it. She didn't know how to get rid of it.

I said: "Listen, it is not as bad as you think. Since the world began women have been at some time of their lives in your situation. And men too, often see the feminine form. It is not a catastrophe, there is no reason to be frightened. The trouble is that no one has told you that it is natural, nor have you been taught how to understand it, and that is why you are in this state. Nature gave imagination to boys and girls so as to make them stir and seek, otherwise it would be the end of humanity. But because of their odd education, it makes many of them lose their health. I am going to give you some advice, and you will get well, not only well, but you will make a great stride forward spiritually. Look, it's simple.

What is this image that you see everywhere? Nothing other than the eternal principle, the active, dynamic spiritual principle of the heavenly Father who created the world. It is an image given to you so that you will be stimulated to make a wonderful discovery. Why not therefore, each time that the image appears, connect yourself immediately with the Heavenly Father? A few minutes later you will have forgotten how it all began and you will be projected up into the sublime regions. There, instead of being upset, everything will be put to use. The bad side of this whole thing is to remain fixed on the image and to lose your head instead of using it as a means of climbing very high and very far. That is the real danger." And I repeat this to everybody: in Nature things are simple, it is humans who complicate them and make themselves ill. What is wrong about the sexual organs? Do you know how much time it took Nature to create them? They enclose the most profound meaning and beauty – All life is there! Why do you tear down the work of God and replace this splendour by your own personal lucubrations? "But," you say, "if you want to be pure you mustn't think about those things." What is pure about going against Nature? You have always been told you must fight against sexual force, but here we give you other methods which consist simply in knowing how to find the beauty and the intelligence which exist in everything.

Today people reject all the rules, all the laws, but show me someone who has gained freedom in this way. The new method, my dear brothers and sisters, is simple and intelligent; it creates no conflict, no tension or maladjustment, and by applying it we will always be amazed at Nature's intelligence in creating the organs of men and women, because when we reflect on these things we go back to the origin of things. Thanks to this method, we feel a harmony, an enlightenment and a peace that makes us burn with the desire to give all this joy to the entire world. That is how to evolve, instead of growing bitter as do people who are unable to solve their sexual problems. Once you have understood this, all creation and all creatures will bring you such a joy, you will see the glory of God in everything, everywhere, and you will live in purity, since you will be asking for nothing more than to distribute this joy that overflows in you.

Videlinata, March 22, 1975.

Chapter VI

Manifestations of the Masculine
and Feminine Principles
I

In the presence of the masculine principle, even at a distance, the feminine principle will react and start to work, and the same applies with the masculine principle in the presence of the feminine. They are both powers which when confronted with each other set out immediately to do a determined work. Men and women are for the most part unconscious of this, it is instinctive with them; they run about searching for each other and they embrace without ever trying to understand why Nature has given them these mechanisms and how they might also be applied in other regions.

The masculine and the feminine principles act on one another in a determined way, and even if the man and the woman notice nothing themselves, the action is taking place: the masculine principle becomes active and dynamic and willful and the feminine principle becomes receptive. This happens automatically in all normal creatures. Initiates who delve more deeply into the reasons for all such phenomena, know how to use the same law on the spiritual plane in order to awaken certain qualities. It is no longer a question of men and women but of divine principles. When he seeks to develop in himself the feminine faculties of receptivity, humility, gentleness, kindness and obedience, the Initiate, who is a man, attracts the feminine principle by joining himself to the Heavenly Father. To develop his strength and will power, he attracts the masculine principle, by joining himself to the Divine Mother. Thus developing the

masculine and feminine qualities within himself, he becomes a
perfect being.

How many times do we see this in everyday life! The feminine
principle makes the boy chivalrous and brave; in the presence of
a girl the greatest coward feels himself to be a knight, and
assumes an air of importance. You say it is bluff, and perhaps it
is, but why this need for bluff? Why does he need to be a hero?
Because of the girl. Look, a husband comes home and tells his
wife that he has met so and so who has told him such and such.
"What?" says the wife, "but you should go and beat him up, he's
an idiot!" "Very well," says the husband to show that he is no
coward, "he will see what's coming to him!" He drinks
something to give him courage, and leaves . . . But on the way, his
courage evaporates, and he returns home saying to his wife: "I
went but he wasn't there." And the wife believes him and marvels
at the heroism of her husband.

Why does a man need to show off in front of a woman?
Instinctively he knows it is the way to win her . . . Because the
woman, who is weak, admires strength, she needs to lean on
someone who is very strong. In the Middle Ages when there were
tournaments, it was the woman who gave the prize to the
victorious: a smile, perhaps a rose. At that time, women admired
heroism and heroes who returned from combat covered with
glory. The same thing is true with animals. When animals fight
over a female, the female chooses the winner, the one who is
stronger and braver. Women don't like weaklings. Of course
there are exceptions, some women are so charitable that they
prefer to have weaklings to protect.

Let's look at the way in which cosmic Intelligence has
separated the two principles; they are different in every way, in
the way they act, in the way they look, speak and work.

Everything that is hollow and deep in Nature represents the
feminine principle and everything that rises up represents the

masculine principle. But when they use their voices to sing, men have the lower voice and women have the higher voice. Why? Because what is below has a tendency to look up. If you are already on the heights, you can't look any higher so you look down, and if you are below, you look up. This is true in other ways: A poor man reaches out for riches, the ignoramus reaches towards knowledge, the enfeebled towards strength etc. Thus woman, who represents the depths, who is the abyss, the void, reaches towards plenitude, she reaches towards the heights, she looks up to Heaven to see her beloved, and he leans down towards her. That is why his voice has become deeper, his natural tendencies show in his voice.

Have you noticed for instance that when a man and woman embrace, the woman lifts her arms to put them around the man's neck, while the man puts his hands lower down? I am not speaking of these details to lead your imaginations onto scandalous subjects, no, what interests me, is the philosophic side and in these gestures that the man and woman do instinctively, I can see significant details. The woman is the reflection of matter, she wants to evolve, to lift herself up, whereas the man who reflects the leanings of the spirit, wants to descend in order to explore the depths.

You can also see a difference in men and women's actions. The man is more creative and the woman is more formative, it is she who fashions. For the birth of a child, for instance, the father is the creator who gives the grain, the spirit, and the mother gives the material which forms it. Man creates and woman forms. The creator of a house is the one who makes the plans, the architect, the house is not yet visible or tangible, it can't be lived in, but it is in someone's head. It remains to be formed with the help of all kinds of matter. Creation precedes formation and it always takes place above, in the head, on the mental plane.

When God created the world, the Creation was instantaneous. It was the formation that took time, and it was then that time appeared. That is why they speak of the six days of Creation. Of course, six days are symbolic, but actually these six days represent the time it took for the formation, whilst the Creation was instantaneous, it is eternal.

And why is it woman's instinct to introduce her tongue into the mouth of the man when they are kissing? It is simply to show that what happens below in the physical world is the opposite of what happens above on the astral plane. On the physical plane it is the man who is emissive and the woman is receptive; on the astral plane it is the man who is receptive and the woman emissive. On the astral plane, the man receives because that is where he is weakest; in the realm of feelings the woman shows that she is stronger. Above it is the woman who gives and below she receives. Whereas the man gives below, and above he receives. This inversion of polarization on the different levels is a profound mystery, and many are mistaken when it comes to interpreting the invisible world: they don't know how to reverse things, and they confuse all the planes. Clairvoyants say that on the astral plane figures, forms, shapes and numbers are reversed, and besides, this is a known fact: people who have been saved at the last minute from drowning all tell of seeing their past lives before them, backwards, in reverse. This is a sign that they were entering the other world, and in that other world, everything is reversed.

That which is below is like that which is above; above in the head, in the mouth with its tongue and lips, is like that which is below, the sexual organs. The words 'above' and 'below' which Hermes Trismegistus used give us only the vaguest idea. In every domain we must know the 'below' and 'above' which correspond. Heaven and earth (or Heaven and Hell), the brain and the sex (or the brain and the stomach), . . . everything which is below is like everything which is above, but in reverse. And even in the anatomical structure of the man and woman, we find this inversion: with the man everything is on the outside, visible, and with the woman, everything is on the inside, hidden and mysterious.

Now, take a young girl, supposedly candid and innocent, who inveigles a young man into sleeping with her, supposedly without meaning to . . . How will she behave afterwards? Weeping and wailing, she will tell him that he has taken advantage of her, that she is sorry it happened until the poor boy, if he is honest, tries to make repairs, and commits himself with promises of marriage or whatever. Secretly the girl feels triumphant because that was what she wanted all the time. Of course there are cases where the boy escapes leaving behind the poor girl pregnant, but that is not what interests us today.

Actually if we study the structure of the woman's sexual organ, we see that everything in her is made to hold the man and make him her prisoner. The man thinks that he is the conqueror and the poor woman his victim. Not at all, is it she who holds him, she restrains and limits him, she makes him her slave and so it is he who is the victim. Only in appearance does the woman accept and submit. Actually she wants to hold him so that all her life he will continue to satisfy her and work for her. And just one more point: he is impoverished, he has left something behind, he is diminished, but she is enriched, she has received a grain of life, and the work now begins inside her. Yes, appearance and reality . . . the man feels proud and the woman, not so proud. Deep down she feels prouder than he, only he is naïve, that's all.

This is the way everything is in Nature. If you try to catch a bird, or an insect, a butterfly, you must envelop it, wrap something around it, you must grip it and clasp it and hold it. The human being who lives in the midst of Nature is dominated by her, Nature is around him like a house, and when you go into a house the doors can close on you, and you are imprisoned, you are a victim. The one who is the master of the situation always holds the other one at his mercy. This is what happens with the man and woman. She is the stronger of the two, because she dominates him and he is at her mercy. The woman needs man, and to attract him, she plays the role of victim, feeble and tender and delicate and timid, because she knows instinctively that the man likes to think of himself as strong, as the hero, the conqueror, but all the time it is in order to get him, to obtain from him what she really wants.

Actually both belong in the same boat because both of them have their schemes. Ordinary love is a battle, each tries to conquer the other. In appearance there are smiles and kisses and friendship, but it is really an implacable war between the two sexes, a well hidden war, of course, because to win over the adversary one is obliged to be diplomatic, and it is not until years later that it becomes plain which was the cleverer of the two. You say: "But what you say is frightful!" It is the truth save only in the case of a man and woman who have a philosophy, an ideal, and wish to work together for the Kingdom of God. Then they are collaborators and not disguised adversaries. Then they both consciously use the different qualities that Nature has given them.

If in appearance man is the aggressor and woman the victim, it is because man is the one who is active and self-willed, with him nothing is hidden, he is exposed and he is unable to hide his feelings, whereas a woman is so constructed as to be able to hide everything, no one can tell what is going on with her. That is why women feel at home with deceit. They are able to deceive, dissimulate and conceal with ease, and to them there is nothing dishonest about it. She waits for the man, and when he arrives she pretends to be surprised, or she pretends not to see him. A woman never shows what she is thinking or wishing because she acts the way she is built, with everything turned inside. Man has on the outside what the woman has inside, in reverse, and in being deceitful woman is merely obeying her nature. Whereas when a man obeys his nature, he is direct, without camouflage, and often even brusque and clumsy.

These little details are anatomical, physiological, psychological, even diplomatical, and they are most important in the understanding of the character and behaviour of men and women.

I will end by saying that men and women must work to develop within themselves their complementary principle. The woman must develop the masculine principle and the man must develop the feminine principle. When I was in India, I visited numerous temples and in all of them, even the smallest, there was always a representation of the lingam, the symbol of the union of the two principles. Sometimes I would talk with the yogis, and ask them: "Have you really understood this symbol?" They would stare at me, outraged. How could a European have the nerve to ask if they understood the symbol that had been part of their tradition for thousands of years? "Very well", I would answer, "but then why do you do the contrary to what you have understood? You are married, and of course it isn't wrong to be married, but it means nevertheless that you are looking for the other principle, the feminine principle, outside of yourself, in someone who is separated from you, a stranger, when this is the symbol that shows you that the two principles should never be separated. The symbol of the lingam represents a being who is perfect, androgynous, and who possesses the two principles at the same time. Since you must look outside of yourself for what you are lacking, it suggests that you have not understood the symbol." They would look at me as if they were hearing these truths for the first time. Some of them would start to ponder, and some would show they were not pleased.

The disciple must work to manifest the qualities of the two principles: the strength, will, resistance, stability, activity, dynamism, and ambition of the masculine principle, always seeking to dominate, to take the lead and to assert itself; and the suppleness, and delicate charm of the feminine principle which submits and sacrifices itself. When he possesses within himself this dual nature, the disciple is a perfect being, called in the science of the Initiates, the androgyne. To be androgynous is the ideal of all Initiates whether they be alchemists, or kabbalists, etc., so as to possess the two principles in abundance like the Deity. In the Deity both principles are united, that is why He can love all His creatures, and be indulgent, and grant their prayers. He has been presented as a terrible father, a consuming fire, but it is not true, He is at the same time both Father and Mother.

Le Bonfin, August 27, 1967.

Complementary notes:

Many musicians, including those who make a study of the theory of music, haven't paused to reflect on the profound meaning to be found in sharp notes and flat notes. A flat diminishes a note half a tone, and the sharp on the contrary, augments it a half tone. Sharps and flats are like the two principles who created everything in the universe: spirit and matter. The spirit descends, goes downward, and the masculine principle always looks downward. The feminine principle which is below, always looks above and must lift itself up in order to rise. The feminine principle is linked to the process of evolution and the masculine principle to involution. Sharps and flats are symbolic of the two principles not only because of their form which suggest the sexual organs, but even more because of the role they play in the scale of raising or lowering the notes a half tone.

The spirit descends into matter to touch it lightly, to water and revive it, giving it new life. This is also what man does during love, he descends towards the woman, and in his descent he loses something, he weakens himself, and feels depleted, while the woman receives something, she rejoices, and blossoms forth and soars like the sharp note in music.

Sèvres, May 30, 1965.

II

I would like to add a few more words to what I told you this morning.

I was saying that the man must know how to become a woman, and the woman should know how to become a man, not on the outside of course, but in the attitude, in the thoughts and feelings, in the way of acting. Knowing how to become positive or negative, emissive or receptive, active or passive according to circumstances, will permit them to solve many problems.

Take the case of a family: the husband comes home unhappy, he is furious because his boss was unfair with him, and at the slightest pretext he loses his temper with his wife. If she is wise and reasonable, she will become at once passive, receptive, she will not answer back, but remain very calm and quiet. He will calm down then because there has been a magnificent exchange between the positive and the negative. If she knows how to polarize herself, the woman can absorb these energies, transform them and give them back to her husband in a way that will make him able to see better, to rise. And the opposite also, when it is the wife who rages, the husband should know how to become negative. Yes, but unfortunately they are both ignorant of these possibilities and when one loses his temper, the other imitates his violence and they create the quarrels, the beatings, the separations . . .

Whether he is man or woman, the disciple should know how to be both at once.

Again: you go to see a Master, and you are emissive, you talk, you explain everything to him as though he were ignorant, and the Master must listen to you ... You should do the opposite! When you are with a Master or someone of tremendous value, you must become receptive, be quiet, and listen so as to learn. And afterwards when you are with people who are dishonest and full of vices, you should become positive, not only so as to receive nothing from them, but to throw out the negative and give them something good in its place. Next to the source, the Master, be receptive. A lot of people have come to me and talked so much that I couldn't get a word in, and then they left, happy at having been able to empty themselves somewhere. I wasn't able to help them, I had no chance, they were too full of themselves. An Initiate knows that he can't do anything with people like that, he can neither use them nor enlighten them. The two principles must be studied: when to be positive and when to be negative.

Tell yourself that if you are unhappy and have no success whatever, it is because you don't know how to work with the two principles. If you have troubles, it is because you have attracted them, you polarized yourself in such a way as to attract them. You must change the polarity and send them away. You must learn how to rid yourself of the evil you attracted and how to attract the good you have repulsed, not realizing it was good.

God has given us the solution to all our problems, but as we don't know how to read or interpret signs, we can't see the solution before our eyes, all around us, in Nature herself.

Le Bonfin, August 27, 1967.

Chapter VII

Jealousy

One often finds jealousy amongst lovers. Wealthy people are jealous too, of their possessions, which they try to hold onto right up to the end, and they suffer at having to leave it all to their heirs. After death, they sometimes return to their homes, or their land, to which they cling and which they had to leave behind, and continue to protect them and worry over them. As they can't cut the ties with this world, they are unable to rise to the higher regions, and remain hovering around their estates, resenting those now in possession.

The jealousy that exists between lovers is even more strange. It is the reason for endless misunderstanding and trouble and it does nothing but make their lives miserable. How many couples come to see me, the husband accusing the wife and the wife accusing the husband – of infidelity! And when I examine the situation, I find it is all purely imaginary. In the end, why all the fuss? They are afraid of losing their darling and yet with what pleasure and delight each troubles and tortures the other! "It's because I love you that I torment you, darling . . ." What logic! Often a wife will be discontented and unhappy because her husband is not jealous. She can see that he loves her, he deprives her of nothing, he gives her plenty of freedom, and instead of being glad, she worries and suspects him of having a mistress. Must he keep her in chains and behave like a dragon for her to be happy? Human nature will never be content, believe me. If a husband gives his wife freedom, she laments: "Why doesn't he worry about me? He must have another woman." And if he's a tyrant and a despot with her, she goes off weeping in search of another man to set her free.

It is when we are afraid to lose something, when we want to keep it for ourselves and not give it to others that jealousy appears, along with the fear of losing this thing which supposedly belongs to you. But where does it say that your wife, or husband, belongs to you? You've known them for two years, or ten years, but they were created long before you knew them. They have parents, and their Creator, and they've existed for thousands of years; they do not belong to you. A husband will say: "She's my wife, I can kill her if I wish." Yes, she's your wife, but for how long will she be your wife? God knows. You are associates, that is all. If you wish to avoid serious misunderstandings, and even great unhappiness, consider her as an associate – voluntary or involuntary – who knows? You have associates to help you undertake a job like building a house for instance, and when you bring a child into the world, you are building a house, the child is a spirit come from far away, and you build him a house, brick by brick.

The fear of losing one's possessions is the reason for all misunderstandings. You are afraid of losing someone you love whom you imagine you own, but he doesn't really belong to you. You use every means to hold on to him, you torment him and browbeat him, you try to impose your will on him, but all of it creates nothing but disorder. And actually, what do you hold on to by acting in this way? Suppose you have a beautiful wife, can you keep other men from looking at her, from admiring her and even from following her? The opportunity is not lacking, whether in the street, at the theatre, in society, amongst friends, everywhere, the entire world will stare at your wife, and if you are not reasonable, you will suffer. You are like someone who has flowers in his garden: he can't keep their perfume from spreading around and being breathed by everybody. Actually, what you are guarding so jealously is the body of your beloved, the envelope, the shell . . . What constitutes the true, the real treasure of a human being, his essence, or his thoughts, his feelings, can never be confined. The greatest illusion is to imagine that one can dominate the human soul. It is like trying to tie up the sand or the wind. You can't have dominion over the soul. You can manage to take possession of the physical body, but not of the mysterious being who lives within the body.

There have been people who tried to keep a hold on a man or woman with magic, which is possible. There are all kinds of formulas and magic processes to cast spells on people but I don't advise anyone to use them. Why? Suppose you were able to force a woman to love you. She might even fall madly in love with you, everything under the sun is possible. But when that woman kisses you and gives you what you are asking for, you don't know what else she may give you at the same time. You don't know what she may have inside, what spirits you have evoked. You must know that it is spirits, summoned by your formulas, that have installed themselves in her; it is not her spirit that loves you, but lower entities, who, if you could see them, would make your hair stand on end, and you would beseech Heaven to set you free. To use magic on people is not a good method. Of course, you will be able to have what you want, but while you think you are tasting love on the woman's lips, you will actually be tasting the poison that will eventually destroy you. You can conjure up the entities from the astral world and make them do what you want, but the Spirit is free, and can never be bound or tied.

So what is the fear of losing a shell, the body of a person, one's house, next to the joy of winning someone's spirit, of having that spirit by your side? You'll say that it is better to have both, the body and the spirit. Yes, I see that, only there are other ways of obtaining them. It is neither with anger nor violence that you will succeed, on the contrary, by these means you will lose both. You must adopt another attitude so that this free spirit will be so attached to you that nothing will separate you. The knowledge of love begins here. There is only one way of making someone love you of his own accord, without forcing him, and that is never to think anything bad about him, to send him nothing but the purest, brightest and most splendid thoughts. Even if he is mean and difficult, be very patient, accept everything and go on helping and loving him. If you really want him, sooner or later he will begin loving you, and his love also will be pure and divine.

Jealousy is very difficult to overcome, and it can't be done simply with effort. As I told you yesterday, nothing can be done against a force that has already been released for it must take its course and upset everything in its way. Don't try to change the course of a river when the flood gates are open, it's too dangerous, it carries everything along with it. The only thing you can do is not to open the flood gates, then yes, you are master of the situation. The only thing that can conquer jealousy is intelligence, for the key to everything lies in one's way of thinking.

Someone will say: "Yes, but if you aren't jealous and if you don't watch her carefully, she will make a lot of mistakes." Don't believe it. It is when she is too closely watched, when she is watched jealously, that she will make the most mistakes. Are you inside her head and heart to see what she does? A wife is so adroit at lying that she could fool God Himself, and some idiot of a husband thinks he can hold her! If there is one thing I do not believe, it is that any man can keep a woman against her will. She can control herself, yes, but her husband cannot. If he shuts her up in a tower, she will summon the devil himself and distract herself with him to punish her husband.

Jealousy always brings catastrophe in its wake. By dint of hearing herself accused: "You're unfaithful, you're unfaithful . . ." the wife finally says to herself: "Let's see, it might be interesting!" Up to then she was faithful and had no thought of cheating, but he, because of his suspicion, creates the right conditions on the astral plane, and from the moment she decides to do so, not only is she unfaithful, but she is expert at calming his doubts: "Darling, you can rest assured, I always tell the truth . . ." and he who didn't believe her when she was telling the truth, believes her now that she isn't.

Jealousy denotes lack of intelligence. We persist in holding on tightly because we can't see that the one whose body we are guarding so jealously, has a soul and spirit that are absolutely free. If you see that there is something finer and more subtle in people on which to base your relations, you will begin to grow, and the methods you use in regard to the person you love will become more sensitive and more intelligent. The person will then become much more attached to you because he will see that you are reasonable, you don't impose on him, or her, and that he can have confidence in you. When fear leaves, you stop being tense, vulgar, mean, and vindictive, you become quieter and learn to handle the problems that present themselves.

Suppose your wife no longer loves you. Say to yourself that this soul is free, that she was not given to you for all eternity, that before you she has loved a hundred husbands and will love others after you. Why worry if she no longer loves you? Will you always love her? Have you loved her ever since the Creation? No. Well then, calm yourself and know that it is unfair to exact something from her that you would not expect of yourself.

Jealousy is a dreadful feeling that makes the spirit grow dim. It is an evil counsellor and it pushes people into hellish acts that they later regret, but it is then too late. You can kill your beloved in a fit of jealousy, and then weep over her and end up killing yourself.

I will now add something that you have perhaps never noticed. Jealousy drags people down into the lower regions of sensuality. After a jealous scene there follows an outburst of sensuality more violent than ever before. If you don't want to come under the influence of this kind of sensual love, don't manifest jealousy, for you will become entangled and you won't even know how it happened. How many men, after a terrible scene with their wife or mistress, after swearing to abandon them, have given in to an irresistible sexual urge and have humiliated themselves in order to obtain a single caress!

A disciple should leave jealousy behind, it wouldn't be right for him to go on with the same worries, the same distress as before. If his wife leaves him he should say to himself: I am sorry to lose my wife, I know it's going to be hard and I have suffering ahead of me, but I also have all of Heaven, God, the light of the Teaching, the Maitre . . . I am therefore rich." If you have only one loaf of bread, you will not feel like being generous, but if you have several, you will give them cheerfully knowing that there will be enough left. Jealousy is a sign of poverty. If you are rich inside you are not afraid of being left alone, and even if everybody leaves, you know that hundreds and thousands of spirits will come to visit you.

One of the most efficient ways of freeing oneself from jealousy is by learning to lift one's love onto a higher level. Why does a woman who loves a man for his mind, his knowledge, his spirit and his kindness, want the whole world to recognize him? Why is she happy when everybody gathers around him? Because hers is another kind of love, far superior to ordinary love, the physical love that makes a woman love a man for his little moustache or his big muscles. What matters is to know how to transform one's love; if it is sensual, you can be sure that jealousy is inseparable from it. Yes, if you love someone purely physically, if you want him to belong to you only, jealousy is not far off: and the more spiritual your love is, the more you want to give to others.

A woman should never marry a man who is much younger, because she is asking for trouble. It is more normal for a young girl to love an older man, because men don't change physically as quickly as women. When a woman is unwise enough to fall in love with a younger man, she will one day see the young man leave and go in search of younger game and she will be unhappy. We must not put ourselves in this kind of situation.

Do not let it surprise you that I often speak on the same subjects. They must be understood not only in theory, but they must be put into practice. For seven years I have spoken to you on the same subjects, presenting them in different ways, especially on the subject of love, because I see that you are always struggling with the same difficulties. When I see that you have resolved your problems, I will turn the page, and if I see that the collective consciousness has raised its level, I will reveal new things, but until then, it is not more knowledge that you need. Take only one talk in which the principles of the Teaching are set forth, and even if you work on nothing else your whole life, it will become clearer and brighter. As long as you only look for facts and theory, you will always have the same problems. You should now try to realize everything you have learned in theory, and you will see a new world opening before you.

Sèvres, March 24, 1945.

Chapter VIII

The Twelve Doors of Man

I have already spoken to you about the twelve doors of the
New Jerusalem, showing you that they represent, symbolically,
the twelve doors of the human body. Where are these doors?
First, there are the seven doors in the head: the two ears, the two
eyes, the two nostrils, and the mouth. These doors are open, they
all function, but for the moment and for most people, they
function only on the physical plane. We must now develop the
ears, eyes, nose, and mouth on the spiritual plane. When we
become clairvoyant, and clairaudient, when we begin to breathe
in, consciously, the fragrance and flavour of the divine world,
when we use our speech creatively, it means that we are opening
the first seven doors.

Let us now take the five other doors. There are two on the
breast, open in the woman for her to give milk to the child, and
closed in the man. There is another door at the level of the solar
plexus, the navel, which is closed in most cases, but when it is
opened spiritually, it is a means of reaching the higher planes. As
for the last two doors – to mention where they are is unnecessary
– at the moment they too function only physically, and we need
to open them spiritually. For instance, with the man, one of these
two doors is used both for procreation and for elimination, but
from an Initiatic point of view, this door has five other functions
with which to solve certain problems and to accomplish certain
things that are still unknown, which make seven in all. You say:

"Five other unknown functions? Oh, tell us about that, it's interesting!" It is too difficult to speak on this subject, because most humans have been imbued with wrong ideas since their childhood, and it would be dangerous to reveal these things at this time.

However, I can tell you that with these twelve doors we can accomplish a tremendous work, for Nature had something in mind when man and woman were created, and now she is waiting for the time when they will be mature enough to reveal to them new ways of being creative. Men and women don't know that they hold the keys to all the mysteries of life, the instruments which will permit them to realize the most extraordinary creations. They don't know how to proceed yet, but when they are ready, these revelations will be given to them. Humanity is predestined to know about these twelve doors, to investigate them and to discover the wealth hidden behind them.

When we use the word door, it always implies a passage, a way of reaching somewhere. Doors are made for a reason, except in the theatre. In principle, a door allows one to enter a new region, a temple, or a palace, a city, there to discover hidden treasures, or perhaps things terrifying to behold. In fairy tales there are always doors to open or, on the contrary, doors not to be opened for fear of the monsters on the inside that threaten the life of the hero. It is a fact that there are some doors that are better left shut, that must not be opened prematurely.

The Kabbalah speaks of fifty doors. The twelve doors of the New Jerusalem I mentioned to you a while ago, correspond to the twelve signs of the Zodiac, but in the Kabbalah, the doors are the doors of Intelligence, placed in Binah, in connection with the sephirotic Tree, the Tree of Life, and there are fifty because each one corresponds to the five regions in each sephira. There are ten sephiroth which makes fifty doors. The Initiate who arrives at perfection can open the fifty doors and help himself to the treasures of the universe stored within since eternity. But to open the fifty doors, they say you must first have travelled the thirty-two paths of wisdom, and that requires strength, and time, and spiritual qualities, and a guide. Twenty-two paths communicate between the sephiroth, for example, the first path which corresponds to the Hebrew letter א, links Kether to Hochmah. If you add the ten sephiroth to the twenty-two paths, you get thirty-two. Taking a path consists in going through certain specific experiences so as to understand its name and its particular characteristics. One can take them one by one, or simultaneously, but it is said that the thirty-second path is the hardest of all.

Let us come back to the twelve doors, in particular to the sexual organs. I was saying that if one knew the five other functions of these organs, one could realize the most extraordinary things. Only, for the moment, I am not allowed to speak on this subject. Furthermore, since the beginning of time, the Initiates have veiled these truths, and even if they also advised humans to hide this part of the body, it was not for reasons of modesty or hygiene, but to show that they should be left in obscurity for they contain too much meaning, too much power. I could reveal a lot of things to you, but I cannot, I will not. I will just reveal one little thing to you that may put you on the track: certain Initiates, who knew how to use these divine forces, used them not for their own pleasure but to do good, and in particular to produce rich harvests, and then a whole population would live in abundance and prosperity without anyone knowing what brought it about. So you see how far removed is this idea from the majority of humans who know of nothing better to do with their organs than to impoverish and empty and unbalance themselves – uselessly wasting all their wealth in trying to have a little pleasure!

You will say: "What? Spiritual work can be done with that part of the body? – Yes, it is precisely there, with that part of the body, that the greatest work has been done! – But they are shameful, nasty, evil . . . – Ah! And is that why children come from there? Why is it that God gave it to these organs to create life? Neither the brain, the lungs, the eyes, the arms, nor the legs can create life. It proves that there is hidden the greatest mystery in existence." Can there be a greater mystery than life? Why would God in His infinite wisdom and intelligence have chosen the worst place for the most precious and sacred thing of all? The time has come to change and correct these erroneous opinions which are the cause of all the abnormalities and disturbances from which humans suffer.

Life comes from our sexual organs, along with inspiration and energy. Man's physical and psychic balance depend on them, they are the factories that make the things humans need most, and yet, they are the organs that everyone scorns and ridicules – because with them men and women lose their heads and get into trouble. Instead we ought to be in awe and amazement at them, and think this way: "My God, what a store of riches You have given me! How can I use them for the good of the whole world?" In order to do that, you have to replace the old words pleasure, voluptuousness, satisfaction, with the word "work", and then everything will be different. You say: "Yes, but if it is work, will I have any pleasure?" More! Your pleasure and joy will be twice, three times, one hundred times greater.

I am not allowed yet to reveal these sacred truths. Nothing is more sacred. Those were the Mysteries: The Mysteries of Egypt, of India, of Greece, of Thrace. There are no other Mysteries, it is they that give access to the knowledge of all other mysteries. They are the Alpha and Omega of sacred science. And when discussing the great secrets of alchemy, the elixir of immortal life, the magic wand, and the philosopher's stone, most people, even alchemists, don't know what they are talking about. When it is known that these three symbols stand for certain truths closely related to sex, there will be general stupefaction. There have been writers who

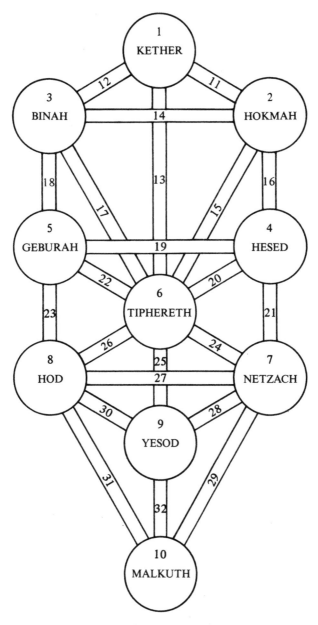

Sephirotic Tree

must have known what the symbols stood for, and who made allusions to them without saying anything more openly. And the Arabs, who were great alchemists, especially those who lived in Spain and founded schools through which their art was made known to Europeans, have a significant word in their language for the philosopher's stone, it is "tachak", which is the word for the two male testes, and which also means rock. Those are the two rocks that are at the base of everything. If I were not sure of being misunderstood, I would tell you what Jesus meant when he said: "Thou art Peter, and on this rock I build my Church". If you knew the alchemic meaning of the rock! And the meaning of "my Church" . . .

Women have no idea of the significance of certain parts of their bodies, nor do they know what they are related to. For example, there is an invisible current of energy which emanates from the breasts, one of which is related to the Milky Way (there have been painters inspired by this subject), and one related to the Moon. You are surprised? These were familiar facts to the Ancients of the past. With some women this current is so pure, intense and luminous that one can't help staring, and with others, their breast can be beautiful and round and pretty, but there is no emanation, nothing at all. If this is so for the breast, why not for the rest as well? And there, some people emanate something really repulsive, whilst with others it can be a clear spring.

I have talked before on the subject of women knowing consciously about the currents they can receive from men through their sexual organs, even outside of any physical contact, and that they must know how to screen themselves off spiritually, because the currents can be bad as well as good, impure as well as pure. The currents men emanate from these regions are sometimes far from pure, and women must learn to be careful and vigilant in this respect. I will also add that these organs God has given to women, can become like radar, a sensitive and intuitive centre, to warn them and inform them as to the nature of approaching people or events. There are women who are evolved enough to notice that it is through this particular part of their body that they are warned of approaching danger, which allows them to take precautions and avoid it. Others, poor things, are only sensitive when they are in bed with someone.

I would like to come back to the door of the solar plexus. It is a most important door which we must open, and through it come into contact with Nature, who feeds us. We live in Nature's womb, like a child in the mother's womb, and we too are fed the things we need, as the child is fed through the umbilical cord. You say: "Yes, but we are already born, the cord is cut." But we are still in Nature's womb and there is another cord which is not cut. I agree that we are already born in the physical plane, but on another plane we are not yet born, we are still being fed through an umbilical cord, and we are still unconscious. To be born, we must have another consciousness, and it will be a second birth, rebirth. The first birth was to cut the umbilical cord which tied us to our physical mother, and while waiting for our second birth, we are tied to Mother Nature through our solar plexus. How many things have I learned through the solar plexus! For years I have worked on my solar plexus, and how many revelations it has brought me!

Everybody knows that to create a child, a man and woman have complementary roles: the man gives the germ of life, and the woman gives the necessary matter with which to envelop the grain, make it grow, and give it a form. Everybody knows this, but nobody knows that women also play a spiritual role. On the spiritual plane, they also give something material, a fluidic matter which serves to make divine creations. With their fluids and emanations, they contribute towards the materialization of ideas, making them tangible, like a child. That's how the ascetics and hermits who fled from women showed that they never understood their true importance. Woman is the key to the concretization of ideas on the material plane. Each woman is capable of emanating this quintessence with which to envelop sublime and divine ideas.

The role of the woman is grandiose. This is why I can appreciate the sisters, while keeping them at a distance, because with their looks and their smiles, they are giving me this quintessence, and I can then go to work with this matter that they emanate, and make the world full of thousands of angelic children! I am not afraid of women, I don't consider them as the devil's work, I consider them divinities. Only women can give me the material necessary to my work, the divine work. Men are different, they can't give me the same material, but they can give other things that women can't give. If all those who were bent on chastity in the past had had this knowledge, with the purity they had, they could have accomplished wonderful things. They will come again, reincarnated, and will learn this way of thinking. Why flee from woman? One must flee from her or one must understand her. I try to understand her.

I will end with something that you must never forget. There is nothing under the sun, in any form, in any way, that has not been contained, synthesized in the feminine and masculine principles. They are a resumé of everything that exists. Whatever you see, or hear, or think, or say, or eat, or drink, or do, wherever you go, there is no one and no thing, no science, no activity that doesn't correspond in the way of function or structure with the sexual organs of men and women. You will say: "You must be depraved to bring everything back to that." It was not I but the Creator who decided that every manifestation of life, everywhere, in all the realms, would be a likeness of these two functions. God took them as models from which he made all His creatures. Reproach Him if you don't agree! Tell Him that it shocks you or bothers you. God doesn't care about what bothers you. He made things thus, and if it doesn't correspond with the principles you were taught, it's all the same to Him, believe me.

You can understand why the Initiates considered these two symbols the most sublime, the most profound, the most significant: all of creation is to be found condensed within them, and all other symbols originated from them. They are sacred to me too, and I am continually amazed at the Intelligence which brought the Tree of Creation out of those two little grains. I invite you also to climb high above, and contemplate this splendour, and learn how and to what purpose, God created these wonders.

When Hermes Trismegistus said: "That which is below is like that which is above," it was thought that by "below", he meant either the earth or Hell, which is not entirely wrong, but he also meant something else which you can now understand. "That which is below" is as intelligent, as glorious, as divine as "that which is above", in Heaven . . . This first sentence of the Emerald Tablet has a miraculous meaning but only those with Initiatic knowledge can decipher it.

Sèvres, January 3, 1965.

Chapter IX

From Iesod to Kether: The
Path of Sexual Sublimation

In the sephirothic Tree of Life, purity is represented by Iesod, which is the realm of angels, as well as the Cherubim who are responsible for life. The pictures of cosmic man, Adam Cadmon, show the genital organs linked to Iesod, purity, because life is created by those organs. For the moment, at least as far as humans are concerned, purity and sexual organs have nothing in common, but for a life of holiness, they must go together. Saintliness is based upon a sound understanding of sexual problems, and not until man is able to control his sexual energy can he become a saint, there is no use looking elsewhere, it is the only way to sainthood.

At the other extreme of the central pillar of the sephirothic Tree is the sephira Kether, ruled by the order of Seraphim, creatures of such purity, such holiness, that they were given the task of glorifying the Lord. It says in the Book of Revelations that day and night the Lord is glorified through the mouth of the Seraphim, repeating ceaselessly: "Holy, Holy, Holy, Lord God Almighty, which was and is and is to come." Holiness, although it is placed very high, depends actually on what is below. Kether, the crown, represents the flowering, the full bloom of the sublimation of sexual energy. The sexual energy that the Initiate has been able to sublimate through his purity, becomes saintliness and is manifested by a golden light over his head. Whatever has become saintly doesn't remain below, it rises and is placed very high above, but it comes from below.

The sephiroth represent the cosmic organs, and Iesod is the

sexual organ of the universe. This is why, when everything is functioning harmoniously in this sephirothic Tree which is man, when he is purified below through the purity of Iesod, the sexual energy which climbs to his head, to Kether, becomes an aura of light. Kether is not the head, but the crown above the head, the halo, this mark of sainthood that can be seen in churches shining around the heads of prophets and apostles and saints.

True Initiates are those who have realized within themselves the purity of Iesod. They have organs that are no different from all men, they may fabricate the same substance, but the substance has been sublimated, and made to rise so as to nourish their spiritual centres, and then to appear above their heads like a shining ray of light.

Sèvres, February 2, 1969.

Chapter X

The Spiritual Screen

Can you feel how pure the air is, dear brothers and sisters, this extraordinary purity in which we are bathed this morning? You are thinking: "Why does he always talk about the weather?" Well, because you don't notice it, maybe. Look at the colours, the light, the clarity and the transparency. I never cease to wonder at the pureness of the sky . . .

And look at that helicopter . . . How privileged he is to be able to come this way. Without his knowing it, from our aura, this cone of light that surrounds us, he has been able to receive something very good to carry away with him. If the pilot was in a state of harmony, he opened the door for every good thing to enter inside, and now he will go and sow the seeds he received. It's as though we had given him a bag full of letters which he will distribute without knowing it. Yes, that is the way it works.

Sometimes on the street, you pass by places where terrible things have happened. If at that moment you yourself are in tune inside with the vibrations that emanate from that place, you will be influenced by them, they can inspire you to evil actions, you too, without your knowing that it was because of the etheric emanations you received while passing this place. We must know how to close ourselves to whatever is negative and open ourselves only to whatever is harmonious and full of light. How does one do this? When I tell you, you will be surprised.

I am always speaking to you about the two principles, masculine and feminine, because they are the key with which to open a lot of doors. You know that it is the nature of the masculine principle to be emissive, and the nature of the feminine principle to be receptive, which explains why a woman is vulnerable, vulnerable to every impure and harmful emanation that tries to invade her, without her being aware of it, through her sexual organs. In her mind, she should install a screen to filter and prevent any but the most beneficent currents to enter. But this is a problem women don't think about, and besides no one has told them before that a certain part of their bodies is like a sponge that soaks up fluids. Women must become more conscious so as to stop receiving the filth that men trail behind them. How often do men walk along the street and stare at a woman imagining what they might be doing with her, and the woman, if she sees him, is flattered and proud of it, because she doesn't know the filth she is accepting.

Women are not able to hold on to their purity unless they protect it. They must become more conscious of the importance of the instruments Nature has given them, and the role they play; they should be thinking and praying and meditating so as not to pick up through these instruments all the larva, the elementals and impurities that will one day ruin them psychically as well as physically. If many women have trouble with those organs, it is because they didn't know the need for a spiritual screen to protect them against the impurities. Instead they consult doctors who have no way of helping them, for they too ignore the fact that it is on the spiritual plane that the remedies are to be found.

It's different for men because their nature is to project, not to receive. And most of the time, instead of consciously projecting only the most vivifying, harmonious and brilliant forces, they project the worse currents and are then proud of being taken for strong males. They project filth into the astral plane and women absorb it and are also proud.

Nature gave six other functions to these organs in the woman's body, as in the man's. For the moment, she can only vibrate on one cord, the coarsest, the others are not yet awakened. Some day she will be able to make the other cords vibrate in tune with the most subtle currents in the universe. She will be the harp of Eolus which vibrated at the slightest breath of wind. When the woman is more evolved spiritually, she will be able to react with the sexual organs to each event, each person. She will discover she has an instrument of the highest precision which advises her as to the good or bad nature of the people around her, so that she can take precautions. For the time being, excuse me, but it is only during relations with a man that the woman's organs react. Women who are more evolved know they have an instrument that informs them about all kinds of things. It is, then, worth while to place a fluidic screen in this part of the body to keep out all harmful fluids.

I am touching on something today that is practically unknown. Doctors study the anatomy or the physiology of the human being, and they know nothing about the other, fluidic side, which is more important. Sooner or later they will have to investigate this field, because they won't be able to go any further, the way will be barred. The only possible issue is the study of man's finer, subtler bodies. For the time being the structure and function of the genital organs of men and women may be well known, but it is only the shell that interests people, and the currents, the forces that circulate through them are neglected although that is what is the essential. Initiates are well informed on the subject of these forces, but nobody is interested in the knowledge of the Initiates.

As I've said, the man is much more protected spiritually, being emissive and impulsive, the currents that circulate through him reject the impurities, and he doesn't attract them the way the woman does. The man attracts them from above, with his head, and the woman attracts them below, and that is where there should be a screen to protect her. I can feel the sisters asking me: "But how do we make this screen or filter you speak of?" With your thoughts. You must pray, meditate, beg the divine world to send you a protector, a being to survey and fend off the impure currents formed by human desires and lusts and passions. If you succeed in attracting a shining entity from the divine world to protect you, you will feel a joy, a purity, an innocence you never knew before, and little by little you will receive the divine spirit and you will become the temple of the living God.

So, exert yourselves, think and meditate . . . During that time, that work, your health and equilibrium will improve and you will understand what purity is; you'll understand that between men and women, everything is a question of vibrations and exchanges and interpenetration on all the planes, but that these exchanges should be on a high plane, of the purest kind, and not only on the lower planes. In this way you will be coming closer to the life of the angels, who ceaselessly meet and unite like rays of light, and in these exchanges, there is no impurity. Ceaselessly, they live in love, above, where only love exists. The life of the angels is a perpetual fusion, an exchange of love in absolute purity. When humans are able to vibrate on all seven of their cords, they will be like the angels. It will be like heavenly music. Blessed are those who have understood.

Meditate on this subject in the greatest purity, in the light, and try to liberate yourselves from the old ideas that keep you from understanding and impede your progress. In this way you will become true sons and daughters of God.

There is of course much more to be said on the subject of filters. There is more than one organ in the woman's body that needs protecting. The disciple knows he is plunged in a cosmic ocean and that he forms his bodies, his physical and his finer bodies, with the help of the good and bad material which he absorbs. The problem he is faced with is to know how to attract only the good, with his head and his heart, and repulse what is evil. Actually, the most effective filter, the one that is the sum of all the other filters, is the aura. If you really want to be protected, meditate on the aura. Imagine that you are surrounded by colours, violet, blue, green, yellow-gold etc. and that these colours form an aura around you, huge, intensely vibrant, radiant, powerful. That is the best filter. Not only will nothing impure, harmful, dark, or evil be able to penetrate it, but thanks to the aura, you will be able to see the splendours of the divine world, to drink and breathe and swim in the cosmic ocean of love and bliss.

To form the aura, it is not enough to imagine colours around oneself, it will last only if it is fed qualities and virtues. As each colour is the symbol of a virtue, the colours of the aura can last only if nourished by the corresponding virtues. For this reason, Initiates have prescribed methods to make the disciple develop the virtues that later turn into colours and lights. And when the spirits above keeping watch over the earth, see among the shadows an Initiate, a disciple, who shines, who sends out beams of light, they come down to him, they take care of him, they water him like a flower, feeding and enlightening him.

So, my dear brothers and sisters, remember that the best protection is our aura.

Le Bonfin, August 16, 1962.

Chapter XI

Nourishment & Love
I

For centuries the Church has been repeating that man was conceived in sin. There it is, nothing can be done about it, man was conceived in sin, born in sin. Well I disagree, I think that by emphasizing and spreading this idea mankind is prevented from righting itself, hopes are diminished and the desire to improve fades. Everybody is sinful, that's all there is to it, the question is settled. Of course there is a truth, but where? Man is conceived in sin, because his parents transmit a heritage that is already at fault. By their thoughts, by their feelings, which are neither pure nor radiant, they have in fact conceived their children in sin. But it is not true that ever since Adam and Eve original sin is passed on from generation to generation. Once men see the light, once they become good, wise, intelligent and pure, whether Adam and Eve committed a sin or not is of no importance, they are changed and transformed.

Humans should not be instilled with ideas that condemn them to feelings of guilt, or imperfection, with no hope of being able to improve one day. We are sinners, that's understood, but we don't have to stay that way throughout eternity, we must advance. Furthermore, Heaven has more confidence in a person who repents than in one who has never made a mistake, because the one who has never done anything wrong is ready to fall, he's not solid, he doesn't yet know what suffering is, he can go off blindly in any direction, and one day, he will fall. But the one who has been in the devil's clutches and lived through dire suffering and has decided to leave that in order to do the will of God, if he succeeds, God will put him to work, He will say: "Finally there is one we can count on, but not on the others." Obviously this doesn't mean you should behave like an idiot so as to be able to improve later, no one knows how many centuries it might take. In any case, humans have done enough misbehaving, it is time for them to settle down and go to work for God.

Take for instance, the question of love.

In the course of time, the conception of love has evolved. The early savages behaved with tremendous violence, an unbelievable brutality and sensuality, and the way they expressed love, without thinking, with no attention, or care, or consciousness, was more like a wild sea or a volcano erupting. With the awakening of consciousness and the life of the spirit, new elements like tenderness and delicacy came into being . . . And yet even now love remains a primitive manifestation. Instinctive passionate love has been the rule for such a long time, that men no longer know how to make love fine and noble. Actually, nothing is harder to do, but also nothing is easier once you know the rules to apply on the different levels, not only for holding someone in your arms, but for love on every plane.

Love is divine life that has come down into the lower regions to take over, to spray love around, to bring all to life. It is manifest everywhere without humans realizing that it is always the same force, the same cosmic energy that has all kinds of aspects. Humans do nothing but waste this energy thinking that it is only an instinct, a moment of pleasure, and a means to propagate the human species. Initiates who have risen above to study the divine power of love, tell us that it is the same energy that comes from the sun, the same light, the same warmth, the same life, but that in coming all the way down to us, like a river, it assumes the impurities of the regions it has to go through. But this doesn't mean that it didn't spring forth pure and crystal-clear at the top of the mountain. This energy which we call love comes from heavenly regions, exactly like the rays and the heat of the sun, but it has become unrecognizable because of its descent into the lower layers, among human beings.

Now the question arises: since this energy is divine, most powerful and most essential, how can it be restored to its original purity? First of all, we must realize that there are thousands of degrees of love, then we must realize that we need to learn control of ourselves, by being thoughtful and attentive and intelligent, for this energy to be once again as clear as the light of the sun, spreading good instead of spreading the forces of destruction. There are rules to know and follow, but to apply them you shouldn't wait to be holding your beloved in your arms, they should be applied to every day life, long before the process of love begins to stir.

Each day you prepare food, and then you eat it . . . you select what is edible, you don't eat everything. Whether fish, cheese, vegetables or fruit, there is always something dirty or indigestible that should be washed clean or thrown away. Man chooses what he eats, he is more evolved than the animal who makes no selection. But when it is feelings and thoughts that are concerned, man makes no selection whatever, he swallows everything. Why? Why should he allow harmful elements to enter his heart and his mind, elements that have not been washed or cleaned? Why, when lovers are about to kiss, do they not think about what they are about to exchange, and remove the impurities? Otherwise, the germs of illness and death slip into their feelings, their kisses, they can't see them and stop them, but they are there. Yes, death enters along with the expressions of sensual love, the brute form of love which is unconscious, uncontrolled, in the dark. That is the kind of love that everyone now sings about and praises and glorifies. No one knows about the other love, and if you mention it, people look at you as if you were mad.

Nutrition is the first step. Before sitting down to the table, people wash their hands, and in the past, they said a prayer inviting the Lord to partake with them. Maybe a few peasants still do that, but educated people are through with such traditions. This is what intelligence and culture have done for people! The custom of washing your hands and inviting the Lord to sit down at your table had a deep significance, and the Initiates who introduced the custom were saying to their disciples: "Before loving someone, before taking someone in your arms, invite the angels to come to the feast, but first wash your hands clean, that is make yourselves pure, have in mind the thought that you want to give the other person nothing soiled, nothing discouraging or sad, no illness." That is not the way it usually happens. The boy is miserable and unhappy, he needs comforting, so he takes the girl in his arms to comfort him. What does he give her, his beloved? He takes everything from her, her strength, her inspiration, and in exchange, he gives her what he wants to throw away, to rid himself of. He shouldn't have kissed her then, he should have waited, he should have said to himself: "I am poor and miserable and dirty, first I will go and wash and prepare myself, and when I am in a better condition, I will bring her all my wealth." No one thinks this way: in the future when these things will be understood, we will be ashamed and disgusted to see with what ugliness we have loved. You will say: "But everybody does that: when one is sad, that is when one needs comfort." Because the world is stupid and selfish is no reason to be the same way. In the future you will learn to love as the sun loves, as the angels love, as the great Masters love, without stealing, without taking, simply by giving.

There are days when you feel poor. On those days, stay away

from your beloved, or else the law will come and ask you to explain why you stole from her. People are extraordinary: when they feel well they distribute their wealth to anyone, but when they feel miserable and desperate, they divest the ones they love. They are thieves, absolute thieves.

In love as in nutrition, the first rule is not to eat the food which is before you without first making a selection. For that you have to know the difference between one feeling and another, a selfish feeling and one that is unselfish, a feeling that limits and one that sets free, a feeling that disturbs and one that harmonizes. You have to be alert to be able to sort out your feelings. If you are carried away and your attention wanders, you will not be present at your frontier to see the enemies trying to slip across and undermine your country. Vigilance, attention, control are necessary in order not to be carried away: but the way humans love, all they want is to be carried away. When they don't think any more at all, when they are unconscious, or drunk, that is when love is best, they say that when they are sober they don't feel much! How do they know? Have they ever tried to be alert and watchful, to be selective of their emotions, and to connect themselves with the higher currents to know what they would feel, and what discoveries they would make? If they have never tried, how can they have an opinion?

I have said that the lower kind of love, passionate love, brings death, and so that it will be clear to you, I will explain with the help of some ideas based on astrology. You know that the Zodiac of the astrologers is a living book in which the Initiates read the great truths of life and the world, and this book is reflected in everything that exists on earth. The twelve constellations are responsible for all the forms of existence on earth. If you want to solve a philosophical problem, you must first look in the book of Nature above, the Zodiac, and this is what I have done several times in front of you. Now, let's take this question of love and death, and let's ask the Zodiac which are the signs that can tell us about love. Actually, many signs speak of love, but particularly

Taurus and Libra because they are the houses of Venus. If you analyze them, you see that Taurus represents primitive and sensual love, the fertility of Nature. The Bull Apis, which was the symbol of fertility, was adored by the Egyptians for the purpose of attracting the forces of the constellation Taurus, through the Bull Apis, so that the earth would have abundant harvests. With magic ceremonies, the priests would be able to draw on this abundance. Venus' other house, Libra, represents love that is pure, the higher form of love. This doesn't mean that all who have Venus in Libra manifest nothing but spiritual and divine love, for there are a good many other negative elements to be taken into consideration, but generally speaking, Libra is the sign of spiritual love, sensitive to beauty, to poetry and music. The Taurus love needs to touch and taste, the Libra love is content with listening and watching.

The Taurus and Libra signs should be studied in connection with their opposite signs for Taurus, Scorpio and for Libra, Aries. Scorpio is connected with the sexual organs again showing the sensual nature of Taurus, and it represents the eighth house, the house of death in Astrology, which shows that, in primitive love when man swallows everything without discernment, the germs of death infiltrate, first of all by discussions, divergent points of view, then by war and revolution. Whereas the sign of Libra is connected with Aries, which represents the head, that is, audacity and courage, the desire to advance, to explore, to climb to the heights, to outdo oneself, to sacrifice oneself. This is why the Christ is represented by a lamb, Aries. Aries is the head and, symbolically, instead of acting with passion and anger, it acts with calm, wisdom and reason. Aries is the beginning of growth and development, the blossoming of everything that grows, that is alive. If a plant grows, it is because it has felt enlightened, it shows discernment, the bad elements are rejected so that life can spring forth and circulate.

Thus, Aries which is linked with Libra, represents spiritual love, in which by the thought which is alert and watchful, the impurities are kept from entering. That is why Aries is the first sign of the Zodiac, the sign of spring, a time for renewal. It is love, the love of the sun, the spiritual love of an Initiate, which springs forth in the form of light, of warmth, of life. This love is pure because it is thoughtful, the mind is present. There are customs formalities at the frontier, and no harmful elements can enter. When you are kissing your beloved, your mind is watchful, you can see exactly what is happening to both of you. You connect yourselves to the higher Intelligence, you make discoveries, and you become powerful. Is it really worth sacrificing these acquisitions so as to be drunk and carried away?

But everyone wants to lose himself and vanish into thin air, because in this way they find happiness. They even tell you so: "If you don't lose your head, you don't feel anything." They are signing their spiritual death warrant, but that is the accepted way. If a man is alert and vigilant, if he controls himself so as to make his love bright and beautiful and good for his partner, she'll no doubt look at him with disgust, thinking: "That's not a man, he is too conscious, he doesn't lose his head." But if she can see that his eyes cloud over, if he breathes hard enough to blow down the world, and if everything in his head falls to pieces, his convictions, decisions, and plans, she says to herself: "Ah, how marvellous, that's really worthwhile. This is a man." It's not that she is so amazed, but she is proud of her power over him, she thinks she has him in the palm of her hand. Seeing that the man is turned upside down, lost, she rejoices, she is triumphant and she thinks: "Ah, he seemed very strong, but now, that's all over, I'll do what I like with him," and her lower nature triumphs, because she will be able to dominate him, to lead him around by the nose so that he does what she wants. Well, this kind of triumph is not magnificent, it is actually cruelty in disguise. The woman should not be happy to see her husband or her love capitulate to that extent. On the contrary, that is when she should worry.

No one is prevented from having intense feelings but we

should be sure of the quality of the emotions and not lose control of them, we should know how to direct things. There are some instruments that are very powerful, the rocket for instance, which, when launched, needs to be kept under control. In the same way, with humans, love can be a fantastic rocket, but it must always be directed, steered, pure and in balance, so that a divine work can be realized. And if that is the moment for them to have a child, that child will be an angel, a genius. There are so many beings waiting on the other side who are evolved, waiting for the right conditions to reincarnate.

You must become vigilant, which means you must light the lights so as to see clearly, and drive off the undesirables. It will take a whole other lecture to show you the effect light has on the astral and mental planes, how effective it is in getting rid of the undesirables. When they try to slip in to take advantage of your energies during love, to eat and drink your strength, you have only to project the light and they won't dare show themselves because they would be exposed and attacked. Undesirables prefer the shadows to glide around in, and that is why you need to be vigilant, enlightened, and informed, to be protected from them.

If, before you take your beloved in your arms, you call on the light exactly as you call on the Lord and invite him to join you at supper, you will be giving her elements that are divine and which she has never before received, and her soul will be eternally grateful because your love is unselfish, disinterested, you want to enlighten her and revive her, and unite her with Christ, to the Divine Mother, and that love is the only love that is constructive. You say: "Yes, but how can you be happy mixing Christ and the Divine Mother with love? It's impossible." On the contrary, only under these conditions will you be happy, because your love will be lasting, you will have neither bitterness, nor regret, nor anguish, nor lassitude. Only a love that is disinterested is without agitation and trouble, otherwise you are like a thief who has taken some money. For the moment he is exultant, but then the question keeps coming up: "Was I seen? Will I be caught?" and he can't be at peace. In inferior and selfish love there is no peace either. You will say: "Yes there is, there is peace." Then you are an animal. The animals are always at peace. Look at a cat, when he has devoured a mouse, how peacefully he licks his chops! But if one is a little bit more evolved, one cannot be so peaceful.

You'll say that I ask you to do the impossible. Yes, I know, but in knowing the truth, the ideal solution to a question, you have already made some progress, even if you don't do any more than that. From the moment we know something to be true, it goes to work inside us, and we come nearer and nearer to realizing the truth. If you don't know what is true, then you will never realize truth, but if you at least know it, then half the work is done because you have an image of perfection, an ideal to follow. There is something for you to look forward to, even though there are still many points to be developed. The question of love will be the big question set before the generations to come. All other questions will fade and the whole world will be busy with the vital question of love, how to love, how to become a divinity through love. Because love is God, God is love. If man's relations with love are correct, it means he has correct relations with God Himself.

When Jesus said to his disciples: "I have yet many things to say unto you but ye cannot bear them now," what was he implying? It was the question of love, he couldn't talk to them about it yet, because his disciples were full of the prejudice they had inherited with the religion of Moses. Take what Saint Paul says on the subject of the way the woman should dress, and submit herself to her husband. Now it is ridiculed, but one day I will explain to you the kabbalistic reasons for giving them these rules to follow, and you will see that for that period they were not so ridiculous. That is among the interesting subjects that await you.

You say: "But tell it to us today!" No, for even on this one subject, I don't know which point to choose. There are masses of things that come to mind, and I will have to make a selection, they are like birds flying in from all sides, and I must separate them.

Jesus spoke to his disciples on many subjects, but he didn't reveal everything to them. He gave them the bread and wine in communion, which was already an Initiation into the knowledge of the masculine and feminine principles, about which the Church is still in the dark. He said: "Whoso eateth my flesh and drinketh my blood, hath eternal life . . ." Where do we find the flesh and the blood to drink? These are the great mysteries that one day will be revealed to the children of God.

Le Bonfin, August 14, 1961.

II

When a man and a woman are loving each other, they shouldn't feel separate from the whole, from the universe and the cosmos, from God Himself. They should bind themselves to the whole, they should be thinking about God and sending Him their forces. If they are thinking about themselves only, they will be sending their forces downward, to be swallowed up by the personality, and they will remain as poor as before, even though they think they nourished themselves on love. Why do men and women seek each other? Hunger is their incentive, they are hungry, they wish to eat. Love is food and drink, comparable to the bread we eat and the water we drink. To love is exactly the same as to eat: the same laws, the same rules, the same processes apply.

Hunger expresses itself in other ways than physically. For instance some people eat their fill and leave the table with a full stomach, but are still hungry, they would like to go on eating but cannot, because their physical body is satisfied, while their astral body is still hungry. Usually the two bodies agree, if the physical body is satisfied, the astral body is also, but when there is an imbalance between the two, either the physical body will need more food even though the astral body is satisfied, or the physical is satisfied while the astral body needs more, creating an anomalous situation.

The same imbalance can happen in the realm of love, when a

person is physically satisfied, sated, but is still hungry on the astral plane. This can be terrible because the physical body can do no more, and yet the astral body remains starved and keeps on demanding more. Some people suffer from this irregularity and inequality between the physical and the astral planes, and they are unhappy because of it. The imbalance can go higher, onto the mental plane....

Perhaps you are surprised that I compare love with nutrition, and draw a parallel between love and hunger and thirst, food and drink, but they come under the same laws. While eating, as I've told you many times, you should set aside everything else and think only about connecting the process of eating with the cosmos, so that all the energies not only nourish your physical body, but are also directed upwards, above. Then the food you are eating will be right, it will be divine and it will bring divine results, your thoughts will be different, you will have other emotions and other impulses for your actions. If you don't understand the process of eating, you won't be able to understand the process of loving, nor the exchanges and relationships between men and women. As long as you eat your food automatically, for pleasure only, without working spiritually at the same time, you will be unable to love as you should, you will always be limited and restricted. Beginning with nutrition, by learning to eat food in a different way, you will also be able to nourish yourself on the divine plane with the emanations and exhalations that spring from the divine source. This is a whole science, a prodigious science, which in the future, humans will be required to study.

If I have been insisting for years on one thing, one little thing: how to eat, it is because I have a reason . . . How many times have I not repeated it! But no one has understood what I am asking. You continue to eat without thinking or meditating, without linking yourselves with God, or even remembering to thank him. Here, I would like this act of nourishment to take place in a way that is truly Initiatic, because that is what will make it possible for you to absorb other, subtler nourishment, the nourishment of the stars, mountains, rivers, plants, trees; the nourishment that comes from the fragrance of perfumes, the sounds of music, the light from the sun. It is all nourishment, it is always a form of food, with the same corresponding laws.

But for humans, the way they eat doesn't count, there are so many more important things! They have neglected the priceless riches Nature has been preparing for them for millions of years. They know they must eat in order to live, but they miss everything, they eat in the wrong way, automatically, mechanically, unconsciously, and they miss everything, they haven't understood. We must nourish ourselves, yes, but the point is to send the energies we absorb back to God instead of keeping them for ourselves, and in that way we develop qualities of generosity and unselfishness. From now on, take all the energy and strength you absorb during the meal and say: "Lord God, come and share my food, nourish Thyself with me", and invite the angels and the Archangels to share with you. This is an attitude that will transform you. When you have understood – for you don't understand yet, I see that you don't – you will have the foundation you need in order to advance in the region of love and emotions. You will feel a light within you, you will be able to go further and further, always following the same divine rules. Instead of wanting to absorb everything and keep it all for yourself, instead of being selfish, violent, and cruel, you will be able to do something really important.

In order to be properly nourished, men and women must learn to feed the divine principle within them, and not the animal or lower principle. For the moment, whether they are embracing, talking, walking, or creating children, they invariably set aside the divine principle and abandon it. It is the last of their worries, and that is why the exchanges they make not only cannot be of any benefit to them but will, on the contrary, bring them worry, sorrow, anger, arguments, illness and emotional disorders and suicide, and naturally, nothing can work anymore for society. Everything is connected and inter-dependent, from the smallest detail all the way up to Heaven.

Learn first how to eat and you will know how to nourish yourself on the other planes. Once men and women begin to nourish themselves divinely, to treat love as divine food, everything will be beautiful and perfect, Heaven itself will stand in awe, Heaven will participate in your love, divinities will come down on earth and walk among humans ... How do you think you can attract glorious entities and intelligences if you are vulgar, ignorant, selfish, closed, incapable of seeing anything at all? What I am saying is terrible, but it is the truth. I must tell it to you, I am here to do just that, for if I never said anything Heaven would not be pleased with me and would send me away. You say: "Yes, but it's not very pleasant for us." It's better to accept unpleasantness and avoid something much worse.

Nutrition reveals all the secrets of the universe. For me it represents a world, an infinite world ... As long as you are in such a hurry, hurried to the point of not taking one hour to eat properly, to meditate, you will be deprived of the greater possibilities of understanding life; and especially, of transforming your sexual energies into light, intelligence, splendour; instead you will always be groping around in the lower regions. As long as you don't relate your activities to the cosmos, you will be nourishing yourself in the wrong way, you will love in the wrong way, and you will have bad results. Whereas if you are connected to the divine world, with the universal Soul, when you kiss your husband or your wife, you will be sowing seeds of light, sparks of light that twenty or thirty years later will continue to work and produce fruit. Simply because you didn't chain the one person you love to your selfish little personality, taking all his strength and afterwards tossing him away like a lemon peel, but you connected both of you to the whole. The power of love is infinite, it lasts eternally when it is understood divinely, together with the whole, and for the whole.

Le Bonfin, August 12, 1962.

Chapter XII

Woman's Role in the New Culture

The Bible says that King Solomon had 700 wives and 300 concubines. It doesn't say why he needed so many women nor what he really did with them, one can only imagine that they were for his own pleasure and that he spent his life in debauchery. Actually, Solomon was a great sage, a magician who knew how to make the spirits of the invisible world obey him. How could he have had this power if he lived a life of debauchery? His relations with women were of an entirely different nature. You have no idea of the important role a woman can play in the life of a man who is enlightened, and who practises divine magic. Solomon succumbed later on, of course, because he was unable to resist or control the forces he released, but at the peak of his reign, he had all power, both material and spiritual. He built the most extraordinary temple, he tendered the wisest judgments, his fame spread throughout the entire world, and his kingdom reached heights of splendour that had never been seen.

Of course, Solomon's splendour was not the spiritual splendour sought by the great Initiates. In the eyes of Initiates, Solomon worked his magic for himself, for his own glory and fame, and he therefore doesn't belong in the highest category of magicians. Solomon is a little like Louis XIV if you like, his magic was not theurgy, divine magic. There are several degrees of magic, and few magicians have reached the highest degree, which requires renouncing their ability to do magic for their own purposes, and relinquishing their power to summon spirits and elementals to carry out their personal ambitions. True magicians refuse all that and think only of the Kingdom of God, they put all their ability and energy and knowledge to work for the realization of the Kingdom of God. They are the theurgists, that is they practise divine magic, for divine purposes. They are free from ambition and they seek neither glory nor enjoyment; their only desire is to transform the earth so that God will come and live amongst humans.

Solomon didn't raise himself to these heights, but he had great knowledge and great learning, and particularly, he knew that woman imparts the substance needed by divine spirit, the substance with which the divine principle creates forms. The divine principle can produce the seed, the spark, the fire, and the power, but these essences are so delicate that they don't take form, they can't be held, they go off and lose themselves in space. To obtain a permanent, real and tangible form on the physical plane, it is necessary for the feminine principle to agree to participate. Only woman, because of her etheric emanations, is able to give the primary substance so essential to the theurgist for the realization of his divine ideas, projects and objectives. A theurgist uses all of Nature's emanations, but he also needs the emanations sent out into space unconsciously by woman. Thanks to her, he can realize his divine magic – without her it is impossible to realize the Kingdom of God.

Women have this indispensable matter which they disseminate in space without knowing it, but if there is no spirit, no divine principle to use it, they will remain absolutely sterile, useless, dry and withered, unable to produce anything whatsoever. They need the divine principle in order to create children, invisible children, thought-children, children in the spirit and soul and heart, angel-children that will bring blessings to all the earth. That is what magic work consists of, the magic work that Solomon was able to do thanks to the energies emanating from the numerous women who surrounded him. He succeeded, of course, but it was not yet divine magic. Divine magic is wisdom. Magic and wisdom are one and the same thing: divine light. But very few beings have risen so high, nearly all of them have used the sacred knowledge to practise sorcery, to acquire money or glory or women or possessions. Whatever may be the practice, if it is to satisfy the personality and the lower desires, it is sorcery. There are many occultists at this stage who may be famous, but are far from being theurgists.

The most sublime magic consists in knowing how to use everything, absolutely everything, for the Kingdom of God: water, earth, air, plants, rivers, rocks, and everything that is emanated by men and women, the unbelievable energies which come from them, which spring out into space without anyone knowing how to use them, or if they do, it is for selfish and personal gratification, and this is what Solomon did. As I have often told you, the personal side is very close to the forces of Hell. Solomon was invaded by diabolical spirits who sought to nourish themselves, and he couldn't get rid of them, they kept returning until finally, he succumbed.

There, let us leave Solomon if you will, and come back to the essential. The essential is that women must understand that they should consecrate the delicate substance they emanate, consecrate their entire being, even their existence, to the divine principle above, so that angels and Archangels can make use of this unique and precious matter, to prepare new forms for the new life. Instead of always putting themselves at the disposal of humans, women should want to wait on God. I present them with this ideal, whether many will come to realize it or not, I don't know. I am here to deliver the invitation.

For centuries man has taken advantage of his authority over women. He has been selfish, unfair, violent, and cruel towards them, and now that they are waking up, they are of course not waking up to enlightenment, but rather to revenge which is no better, even for themselves. On the contrary, woman should be able to forgive man, she who is the mother, she who has more love than man, she who by nature is more indulgent, generous, good, and inclined to self-sacrifice, she must not seek revenge. Woman should awaken to greater virtue, she should rise above her personal interests. All the women in the world should unite for a work of construction, a work to be done on men and on the children they put into the world. Instead of looking at men to seduce them, saying to themselves: "Ah, I am pretty and attractive, and I'm going to take advantage of it..." thus satisfying their vanity, they should lure men into working with them on the regeneration of mankind. Fortunately or unfortunately, there is no question that nature has endowed woman with all kinds of powers, and everything lies in how she uses these powers, for she can also use them to torment man and make him unhappy.

God has given power to man and to woman, but each has a different power. What the woman is able to do, man cannot, and what man can do, woman cannot. Woman provides the substance and man contributes the spirit, that is, life. Everyone knows this is true of the physical plane, but on the divine plane everyone remains ignorant of these great mysteries. From now on, women should unite to create, all together, the collective Woman, who will bring new life to humanity. Without this substance, the divine Spirit cannot incarnate. This phenomenon occurs in spirit seances when the medium is supposed to furnish something of her own substance, an emanation, for the spirits who wish to manifest themselves. The spirits then take and envelope themselves in this substance permitting them to become both visible and tangible, and then they are able to act with considerable power, displacing objects or destroying them. If a medium were to be weighed, the scales would show that she loses several pounds during the seance, and regains them afterwards. It depends on how much substance she has had to contribute.

My dear brothers and sisters, now that you know these laws, you should understand how important it is for you to consecrate yourselves to the divine forces so that they may be nourished by you. If it is said that the human being should offer himself in sacrifice to the Lord, it is so that the Lord might be nourished. Of course, this is symbolic. In certain religions, animals were immolated to serve as food for certain entities in the invisible world. In our day, we light candles or burn incense, or place flowers on the altar, simply because the light, the exhalation, the perfumes serve as food for the spirits of light. Man can go further and offer himself in sacrifice, so that the Lord might be nourished by him, his thoughts, his feelings.

The Lord does not accept us as nourishment unless the plants and trees that grow within us can offer delicious fruit. The Lord will not eat the tree, of course, it is the fruit of the tree He will eat and the tree will remain intact. Our thoughts and feelings are the fruit and He will not come to pick them unless they are marvellous. This is how the Initiates nourish the divine world, they are the fruit trees of the Lord, on which He feeds. As for the trees that produce nothing, they can be compared to the barren fig tree in the Gospels. You remember the incident . . . One day, Jesus and his disciples, feeling hungry, stopped in front of a fig tree, but there was no fruit on the tree, whereupon Jesus cursed it and the tree dried up before them. It is obvious that it was not a question of a simple fig tree, for Jesus would not have been vindictive to such an extent towards a poor tree. The fig tree was symbolic of the Sanhedrin. And when Jesus, the great gardener, came to gather the fruit he was expecting from the people of Israel, they had nothing to offer him and he cursed them. This is also the reason he wept over Jerusalem: "Jerusalem, Jerusalem, thou that killest the prophets, and stonest them which are sent unto thee, how often would I have gathered thy children together, even as a hen gathereth her chickens under her wings, and ye would not! Behold, your house is left unto you desolate." And that is what happened. It could be that now the same thing will happen with the members of the European culture, if they make no attempt to offer fruit to the Lord. But this doesn't even occur to them.

Women must begin to understand the gigantic task they could be accomplishing. They are the reservoir of all the extraordinary matter needed for the realization of Heaven's projects. At the moment they are busy realizing the projects of every imbecile and every criminal on earth with no thought of the divine world. That is where women are. But if they were to decide to consecrate themselves to Heaven so that this marvellous substance might be used towards a divine goal, then all over the earth's surface, there will be homes full of light, the entire world will speak the language of the new culture, the language of the new life, the language of divine love. What are they waiting for? They are forever accepting a destiny that is beneath them, a destiny too ordinary for them. From childhood their only ideal is to make a home somewhere with someone and bring up children. It is they who create for themselves their mediocre destiny, and afterwards they complain: "What a life!" It's their fault, why couldn't they have a higher ideal of life? It would change their destiny.

I am giving you today one of the greatest secrets of Initiatic knowledge. The Initiates, the prophets, the ascetics who refused all contact with women, who failed to understand the importance of her role and didn't know the value of working with her, were unable to realize anything: it is only through women that ideas can incarnate, can take form.

This is why I ask at least the sisters of the Fraternity to consecrate themselves consciously to Heaven . . . Not to me, to Heaven. And through me, Heaven will be able to realize something. Divine consciousness is what counts, not the physical side. I ask nothing more than their presence, their smiles, their glances, their emanations, their good thoughts, their good feelings, and I, with this substance, will go to work. The Divine Principle is needed in order to create beautiful forms in the divine world, only He is capable. A woman cannot be a magus, her nature doesn't lend itself. She is receptive, a medium, a clairvoyant, a prophetess, perhaps a little bit magician or sorceress. But to be a magus, one has to be extraordinarily active and dynamic, one must have the masculine principle in perfect condition and under perfect control. Can a magic wand be used if it is folded in two, or even three? To have the magic wand means that one is active, that one has a will powerful enough to climb to the top, to reach all the way to the universal Soul, and be absorbed within it. How could the helpless, the weak, and the impotent be able to climb as high as the universal Soul and become one with her in order to create? It is exactly like somebody who is impotent trying to have a child. The same laws are to be found on all the planes, and if you are shocked, go and hide your head somewhere, stop up your ears!

Le Bonfin, September 11, 1962.

Chapter XIII

The Initiatic Meaning of Nudity
I

Two years ago, some people who run a nudist camp invited me
to visit it so that I might have an idea of what it was like. The only
one wearing clothes among all those naked people was myself,
and it was I who appeared unusual. Little by little they gathered
around, young girls, women, men, and the strange thing was that
their nudity made no impression whatsoever. I was surprised. I
looked at them, and thought: "There is really nothing so
shocking!" It all seemed simple and natural, the people, their
expressions, everything. We sat down for a moment and carried
on a conversation; several of them asked questions and listened
with great attention. Curiously, several of them said: "From the
way you look at us and speak, we feel that you are a Master. If
only you would lecture to us so that we might learn!" I was
surprised to hear that from nudists. I thanked them but I wasn't
able to stay.

Now you are going to ask whether I am in favour of nudist
camps or not. I am neither for nor against them, but I noticed
that a lot of things were not quite right. I had been told that
nudists were more advanced than other people because they were
free of certain complexes and therefore healthier, better
balanced, and purer. I was interested to see if that were true, and
from what I saw, I realized it was not true. First of all, they were a
bit bored because they didn't have much to do, but especially, as
they had no Initiatic knowledge about the power of the elements,
they didn't receive much benefit from them. I also saw that they
were full of desire and passions which, being naked, they were

able to satisfy. Their nudity therefore was not bringing them any closer to purity. Purity is something more than being able to undress without shame.

Last year I gave a cycle of talks on purity, explaining what true purity is, how to obtain it, the advantages of having it, and the power it generates. Most people think that purity is limited to the field of sexuality. Not at all. Purity includes all the regions, all the planes of our existence. When man thinks purely, he understands; when his will is pure, he becomes powerful; when his physical body is pure, he is healthy; and when his heart, his soul, is pure, he becomes clairvoyant. "Blessed are the pure in heart, for they shall see God", said Jesus. Purity is not only a question of sexuality.

Nudism is expanding all over the world: there are magazines on nudism and articles on nudism, but the knowledge humans have of what nudity means is not sufficient. That's why nudism will not bring them what they imagine it will, it is an attempt that will not go far. What is good about nudists, is that they have understood how important it is to communicate with the forces of Nature, with the air and the sun. Yes, but if they haven't a better knowledge of the structure of the human being, there too, everything will degenerate. Do they know how to expose themselves to the sun? No, they don't; their physical pores may be open, but their spiritual pores are closed because they don't know what it means to be exposed to the forces of Nature. They don't therefore derive much benefit, even by living openly, freely, in Nature's midst. This Teaching throws light on every plane of our existence, allowing us to blossom and giving us the balance and insight that we need. Without a Master, an heir to this science, this knowledge, it would take a long time for humans to penetrate the great mysteries of Nature through trial and error and their own experiences.

There is nothing wrong with nudity, alone everyone can be as nude as they like, it is in front of others that it is not permitted. As humans are not terribly good at controlling themselves, and are neither pure nor intelligent, they had to invent rules to protect themselves. Actually there is nothing bad in nakedness. Ask a pretty woman what she thinks about it. She is so delighted with herself that she spends hours on end contemplating herself in her bathroom. It's when a woman is not pretty and doesn't want to see herself that she turns into a moral person, modest and chaste. Yes, because she's ugly, but if she's pretty, she doesn't think about being moral, she wants to show herself off and be gazed upon and admired.

The need to show oneself in the nude exists in nearly all women. With men, no, they tend to be ashamed to undress in front of people. But they like to see naked women and women like to show themselves. Nature made them this way. Truth tries to show itself naked. If woman and truth were identical, if she herself was as pure as truth, there would be nothing wrong in showing herself naked. But as long as woman and truth are not identical, it is better that she remain clothed before others.

Women have a natural tendency to undress, it doesn't bother them, and the day I went to visit the nudists, I saw young girls who displayed themselves with such candour, I was amazed. They were the picture of innocence! For centuries woman has been told that nudity is contrary to modesty and purity, and still she can't accept this idea – she obeys by wearing clothes, but in her heart of hearts she hasn't accepted, it doesn't correspond with her deepest nature which remains candid and chaste in all her nakedness. It isn't because of depravity or vice that women want to undress, but because they are obeying their nature, and they see no wrong. The idea that it is wrong was added later on. When women saw how weak men are, how troubled by nudity, they realized they could profit from it and now they use their charms to dominate men, to exploit them or revenge themselves.

It is in the use woman makes of nudity that she is reprehensible, not in her natural need to show herself naked. Now it has become so current that it is practically impossible to find anywhere on earth a woman who doesn't consciously use the power of her physical body to lead men around by their noses. And this is why our Teaching also has the task of instructing women so that they will be able to rediscover their true innocence. That they are beautiful, that they have charm, nobody can deny, but, instead of using these powers Nature has given them to tempt man and make him crawl in the dirt, let them use those charms to inspire and raise him up. The power of woman is immense, for evil as for good, but it depends on how she uses her charms, what goal she has, what is her ideal.

But let us return to the question of nudists.

Both the body of man and of woman have etheric antennae, through which they communicate with Nature. When they are naked, they receive the forces and the messages of Nature. Therefore, if they're able to be naked in a forest or by the sea, to perform a spiritual work with the earth, the air, the water and the sun, they will have far more possibility of receiving and emitting currents and thereby obtaining results. Sorcerers, and particularly witches, who knew of the great power of nudity, used it for their magical practices. That is why occult books tell of numerous cases where magicians would remove their clothes before doing their incantations, casting their spells and curses, etc . . .

As nakedness attracts good and evil alike, it is dangerous to expose oneself in the nude if one does not have sufficient awareness and self-mastery, so that one is closed to everything that is negative and evil, and open only to that which is filled with light.

Now, thanks to the science of eternal symbols, I reveal to you the real significance of nudity. To be naked is to be stripped of all erroneous ideas, of all desires. Only truth is naked, so to attain real nudity, one must be free of everything that is dark, thick and vulgar, an impediment for the divine world. When one has reached this kind of nudity, we can then rise to the heights, very high, in order to receive messages and advice – the wisdom, love and help of Heaven.

If humans don't receive much during meditation, it is because they try to rise to the heights without first removing their old soiled and torn clothing – symbolically speaking. How can their antennae receive anything? One must be naked before Heaven, entirely naked, which means stripped of desires, selfish motives, false ideas. Removed of these, we can climb and the more we remove, the higher we climb. And then, we come back down and resume our clothing, our projects and contrivances, which are necessary for the world, but not for Heaven. Heaven approves only of the "naked". You see what a magnificent image the Initiates have given us when they speak of the naked truth, Isis unveiled.

At the present time, because of the disorder and anarchy which reign in all realms of life and culture, there are quantities of powers and entities that have been freed from the underground regions where they have been locked for centuries. Look at what has happened to morals and to art . . . Men have opened the door to the subterranean world, and they have been invaded. To be protected, we must be connected to the Light, to God, to heavenly powers. We must analyse ourselves, control ourselves, and not let go, because by doing so we become like a roadside inn which all the undesirables can enter and go on the rampage. If you don't believe me, life itself will undertake to show you that I have always told you the truth; you will experience for yourselves that hostile and destructive forces exist. Your souls and hearts should be open only to that which is intelligent and reasonable and full of light. You should not let yourselves go, accepting all the madness that comes from the world around you, otherwise it will be the end for you, my dear brothers and sisters.

This Teaching really is something! If you don't apply it, however, the Teaching will always remain marvellous, but you will not. If you take the Teaching and install it within you, it will protect you from all unkindness, from all the unhappy choices you might make, and instead of being in the shadows, always absorbing what is bad and dangerous for you, you will choose what is best, and you will receive every blessing that Heaven has to give.

Le Bonfin, September 12, 1967.

II

If nudism is becoming more and more prevalent today, arousing indignation throughout the world, it also gives us food for thought. How can you prevent people from exposing themselves to the sun in the midst of Nature, and from wanting to rid themselves of their old and hampering traditions? It seems that there are now nudist camps in decent and respectable little Bulgaria! Even Bulgaria wants to be modern. And if the young move more and more towards nudism, why should others wax indignant and tear out their hair? Young people couldn't care less whether people are indignant or not. You say: "Ah, he's preaching nudism so as to prepare us for it, us too!" Not at all, not yet. In a few centuries, when mothers know how to work with their children while they are carrying them so that they will be divinities when they are born, then, yes, people will be able to show their beauty. Why hide something that is beautiful and pure? What they show now doesn't lift people up towards Heaven, quite the opposite. So, not so fast, wait a little, and in the meanwhile, to work! Let mothers learn how to form pure children, so pure and so beautiful whether clothed or unclothed, that mankind will always be absolutely pure. If Nature were asked: "Are you furious that humans are walking around naked in the forests and on the beaches?" – Nature would reply "I don't give a damn. They can be as bare as they like if it does them any good. Furthermore, when I sent them down to earth, they weren't clothed. It is they who thought about it and decided that in order not to be cold, to avoid getting hurt, and to conform to their odd ideas, they should wear clothing, but I planned for them to be naked."

So, if mothers work on ameliorating the future generations, one day humans will be able to be naked all the time. Cities will be heated by solar energy, which will be in use everywhere, and they will go about free and unashamed, filled with wonder. I will also tell you that according to the wisdom of the new Heaven, the Initiates of Greece found that, by knowing how to sublimate sexual energy, it could become a source of inspiration. This is why Greece was able to give us the greatest sculptors, the greatest architects, the greatest philosophers that the world has ever known, who have never been equalled, simply because they knew how to sublimate the sexual force. The Initiates started the custom of festivals during which the most beautiful and the purest of all the young girls danced along the streets, clad in transparent veils, and the men who watched them were filled with amazement at their beauty and grace, at their subtle gestures and attitudes, and this amazement, wonder and energy that gathered within them, rose to their brains and manifested later in the form of extraordinary creations. Thus, even in the past, people knew about the new Heaven, but humans have set all that aside, people have wandered away from such customs. You are thinking that I will advise returning to the ways of ancient Greece. No, I don't advise it, because humans are so backward that the results would not be good. One must have a high degree of evolution to obtain results in this domain, otherwise one is torn apart.

This is the origin of the Vestal Virgins. The Vestals were the most beautiful, the purest of virgins, who danced naked before the Initiates who watched and were inspired by them, but without touching them. To keep these mysteries hidden from the crowd who would not have understood, the story was invented that the Vestals were there for the purpose of keeping the temple fire alive. Does it make sense for them to be in the temple for that sole purpose? The fire that these virgins maintained was the sacred fire of the great Masters. You ask: "Was this fire so necessary?" It was so necessary that without it, even the Initiates could accomplish nothing. The Initiates were old, they never touched the Vestals, but they used their emanations for a work of the highest order of white magic.

The power that Nature has given to women, especially while they are young and pure, is so tremendously effective that even the Initiates have not been able to replace it. They used it to light the fire within themselves, and with this fire they prepared a subtle nourishment which they then sent up above, and in exchange, blessings from Heaven rained down upon their country. It was not for their own pleasure that they projected this force, it was to accomplish a task, in which they took pleasure perhaps, as it is impossible to separate work from pleasure, but it was not their aim. When you are looking for pleasure only, your forces are swallowed up by the earth, whereas when you are working, you feel pleasure and happiness, a sense of unfolding, and your forces are directed towards Heaven, which brings a greater joy than if you were acting for yourself alone, for your own pleasure. It is a joy that is neither degrading nor tiring, instead it is uplifting. But to understand these things, you must have a knowledge of the psychic world.

These ideas on the sublimation of the sexual force come from very ancient times. Unfortunately, afterwards, many of those who practised them were unable to sustain the necessary degree of purity and they fell into sexual magic. They didn't know how to restrict themselves, they went too far, they didn't take homeopathic doses, they took allopathic doses, which affect only the physical plane, whereas homeopathic doses act on the psychic plane, which in turn affects the physical body. In the future, humans will be taught to take love in homeopathic doses, and this amount of love will never tire, use, or debase them, it will carry them straight to Heaven. All who have done what I am talking about were able to rise very high, because they used the extraordinary power of this love.

I can teach you how to nourish yourselves with homeopathic

doses, but I am not sure you will understand. I am sure some of you will be shocked to learn for instance, that I have been known to go to the beach to look at women! You think: "That one can't be an Initiate, we don't even do that, we don't go to the beach to stare at women." Well, I do, consciously, for a reason, and I am not ashamed. I have even taken some of the brothers with me, and I told them: "Try to understand how I look at them, why, and which ones", and they learned that a whole science is contained in the way one looks. Why are all those creatures there? To be observed. But people don't know how to think, and yet, everything is in the way you look at things.

I will teach all the brothers how to look at people, and the sisters too, because they don't know how to look either, they have been fed a lot of wrong ideas that block them forever, and yet they say marriage will save them! Many women are blocked, they suffer because of it, and as long as they don't know how to understand, how to think and look, and how to do everything for the glory of God, they will be vindictive and bitter, jealous and hysterical, forever busy with other people's business, forever criticizing. Women must be saved, and men too, but they won't be saved by the old ideas. The old ideas are good only to give work to doctors and psychiatrists, they will never improve anything, and yet it is very easy, once you change your way of understanding, your way of looking, all the rest falls into place.

You must know how to look and appreciate without destroying the beauty, because beauty was not meant to be eaten, but to be contemplated. In the contemplation of beauty, you project yourself into space and all the rest comes to you – purity, goodness, patience, understanding ... you climb higher and higher and you yourself become a source, a well-spring.

Always look for true beauty, because it will save you by making you choose whatever is bright and pure. When you come across a picture showing a naked woman, you will notice that if her body is perfect, although you admire it, you feel no desire. Artists are aware of this, they know that a slightly imperfect body is more apt to arouse desire. It is said that nudity is chaste. No, it is beauty that is chaste, whether naked or clothed. But nudity . . . When people are naked, it is for reasons other than purity.

So, my dear brothers and sisters, should I go on? Do you begin to feel and understand what true purity is? Purity lies in beauty. You must look for beauty in order to reach purity, because the love of beauty will keep you from losing yourself in places clothed in shadows.

Sèvres, January 1, 1967.

Chapter XIV

Exchanges and Relationships
I

All the world knows that it is usually the man who takes the initiative in approaching the woman. I say usually because from my observation of what happens today, it is more often the girl who makes the advances. But what is normal is that the woman doesn't move and the man, like a hunter, has to go and find her. You say: "But he goes towards her because she attracts him!" It is true, she attracts him, she throws her net around him and pulls . . . he draws near because he is already captured. The girl is like an angler standing on the bank, calmly pulling in the fish on the end of the line. That is how a woman behaves: she doesn't move, the fish comes to her. You say: "But a man can also attract the girl, girls talk all the time about being attracted to a man!" Yes, because man too projects something invisible, but he acts like a climber, a mountaineer: he throws a hook high up into the rock, and then he climbs up. The difference is that he throws something that will help him to make a move toward the girl, and the girl throws something that invites him to move toward her. Both of them attract each other, it is a kind of war, each one has his tactics, but with one goal in view: to be together and make some exchanges.

For instance, at a dance, a party, where boys and girls are together, they look at each other, they exchange a few words, they're happy . . . (don't let's mention those who have some reason to be unhappy or disappointed) . . . between them is a tension which makes them feel light and clear. Nothing happens, they don't even touch each other, yet in the delicate world of emanations they are making exchanges. When men and women sink into the heavier, denser regions of sexuality, what they do physically is simply a concretization of what they have already done on the etheric plane, although unaware that such exchanges were taking place. Men and women are conscious of love only when they express it physically, then they see that something is happening, but up to that point their consciousness is not awakened, they see nothing.

Something else: When someone starts to talk, he is being emissive, and therefore positively polarized, and those who listen to him, either men or women, are all being receptive, that is, negatively polarized. They take in the words and become fertilized, either divinely or diabolically according to whether the words are good or evil. Nature works on all the planes with the same principles, but humans consider only the most concrete planes as those which are real. They are oblivious to, and unconscious of, that which is invisible, subtle, and the origin of all concrete realizations. They don't see, they don't understand. That is where they should be enlightened, their horizons enlarged, so as to be able to catch a glimpse of the glories that Nature has prepared for her children when their consciousness awakens.

Man is emissive through his entire body, his eyes, his brain, his mouth, his hands, and of course, through the organ specially prepared for giving. And woman is receptive through her entire body, but most of all through the place specially prepared to receive. No one can keep them from having etheric exchanges. Why do people enjoy getting dressed up and going out? It is not only to look in the shops and stare at the passers-by. They don't know it, but this taste for going out comes from a profound need. They like to walk in the streets and the parks because they need to make exchanges with Nature and with humans. Exchanges are absolutely indispensable.

"But then," you say, "what about the hermits and ascetics who lived in caves so as never to see either men or women?" They were suppressing certain exchanges so as to have others, to open their spirit to other influences which are less concrete, less tangible and physical. If you are closed to one influence, another one opens automatically. You prefer not to see or hear? Then other eyes and ears will open up in the soul and spirit to become either emissive or receptive. If certain Initiates advise someone to live alone in the forests or in the mountains, it is not to keep their disciples from being emissive or receptive, but so that they will change the plane they are on, and continue being emissive and receptive in other more subtle regions. One is always emissive or receptive, one or the other; if not, one is no longer alive, in which case there is no need for exchanges. Exchanges are the very basis of life, and if one knows how and with whom to exchange ideally, one has found the real secret of life.

I have talked to you about the exchanges we make with solid matter when we eat; with liquid matter while drinking; with air and gaseous matter when we breathe; and finally, with heat and light: the skin absorbs heat and the eyes absorb light. But that is not all in the way of exchanges, for there is the possibility of making many more on other planes. . . .

Unfortunately, men and women have halted on the first rung of the ladder, and they make exchanges only on the physical plane. At that level, exchanges are not divine, they are by nature the coarsest exchanges of all. The science of all these interchanges on the different planes is contained in the symbol of the Aeolian harp, whose seven strings vibrate with the wind. This harp is the human being, man or woman, and each one has seven strings which they must know how to make vibrate. It is not by playing on one string alone that one can learn to be happy, strong and radiant. Men and women are not meant to be monotonous instruments with but a single string. They should vibrate with the six other strings which they have, and which will give them other sensations, other joys, a plenitude superior to the pleasure they

derive from purely physical contacts. But this is really inex-
plicable, you can't explain the sun, or the light, or colors to a
blind man. If they haven't seen or felt these things, it does no
good to explain them.

When men and women are together, a tension mounts in
them, which is normal. Nature planned it this way, but the
question is to know whether this little tension should make them
release and waste their forces. That is where wisdom begins . . . or
stupidity! If they waste this most precious of all energies on a lot
of nonsense, it means they have understood nothing. Nature's
goal was not to push them into getting rid of this tension
instantly and no matter how, but rather to make them reflect on
the reasons for it, so that they might find a meaning and make
use of it to do magnificent things, to send it up higher,
everywhere, throughout their whole body, so that the cells could
be watered, permeated and fertilized. Just because one
experiences a few sensations does not mean that one should
concentrate on them. No, leave the sensations alone, go beyond
them in your thoughts, send the energy elsewhere, towards the
highest point, the brain.

If Nature creates tension, it is not for the sake of destroying it;
without it you may feel more quiet, but you have no more
desires, no more impulsive force, you become completely
deadened, stupefied, because there is no more tension. It is
perhaps all right from one point of view, but then you must be
aware of certain methods to avoid the bad effects on your
evolution. In reality, tension is necessary to bring the water to
the highest floor of the sky-scraper. But to resolve these terribly
important questions, one must study the human being while
thinking of him as something more than a physical body to
satisfy. To have an animal joy, a feeling of relaxation is certainly
necessary or Nature would not have planned it, but not to the
extent of sacrificing all the rest for a purely biological sensation.

The tension is there to bring the energy to the top, but most humans don't realize this and do everything possible to get rid of it because the tension bothers them, whereas Initiates do their utmost to conserve it as long as possible ... for fifty, two hundred years! It is this tension that is important to them, not the slackening, not the relaxation. Relaxation can be extremely harmful. If you don't know how to control this energy so that it will do all sorts of work, put all sorts of wheels in motion, then it will escape in all directions and be the cause of a catastrophe.

But let us return to the question of exchanges. In the living book of Nature, it is written that it is impossible to be pure if one does nothing but take. Purity comes with the need to give, to flow forth ... it is in abundance, in this welling up and out that you become pure, and then there is no law to condemn you. It condemns only if you take, because then you are a thief. Humans call it love, but no, it's stealing! A boy is hungry, he throws himself on a girl crying: "I love you, I love you!" and the world thinks it normal: "He loves her". But the invisible world above says: "He's a thief, he has robbed her." If you take something while obeying only your needs, it shows that you are a thief. You mustn't have the need to take but the need to give.

Actually, there is always one pole that is emissive, and one that is receptive, and that is what makes circulation. When a man and woman are entwined, the man gives the woman an energy which she receives and which climbs up through her spinal column into her head, where, through the mouth, she projects this energy into the brain of the man, who thereby becomes receptive. The man receives above in order to give below, and the woman receives below in order to give above. Woman, so tender, feeble and delicate, is the one who gives on the higher plane. If women knew that, they could transform men by their thoughts. During love, the woman is very strong in her thoughts, much more so than the man, who easily loses his head. The proof is that when a boy and girl are caught in the midst of an embrace, the poor boy stutters and stammers while the girl is in control and is able to think of all sorts of good explanations; never for a minute does she lose her head.

Of themselves exchanges between men and women are neither bad nor criminal. If it were so, why would Nature have shown no other process for the propagation of the species since the beginning of Creation? If the act itself were reprehensible how could Nature have tolerated it, why would Heaven not have exterminated everyone who did it? The act in itself is neither good nor bad, it is the intention that renders it either holy or criminal. To make a comparison: which is more important, the tap or the water that runs through it? The tap can be made of gold, but what if the water it carries is dirty? What counts is the purity of the water. Evil intent is comparable to dirty water, and good intent to crystal-clear, vivifying water. In love, it is neither the gestures nor the organs that are guilty. What matters is the quality of the energy, emanations and quintessences which are present, the qualities of the psychic forces projected by the man and woman who are making love.

If a man has not worked on himself to become finer and purer, if his intentions are selfish or dishonest, and if he gets married for one purpose only, he may be approved and applauded by everyone, his family may hold a feast in his honor, the City Hall may hand him the legal right, and the Church may hand him their blessing, but Nature will condemn him. What will he be giving his wife? Nothing but sickness and vice, the most pernicious influences. The whole world may approve of his action, but the laws of living Nature will be against him, because he will do nothing but corrupt his wife and give her his diseases. And conversely, everybody may reproach you for not being married, but if you have given Heaven to the soul of the woman you love, and if she has become a divinity through you, all the angels above will be filled with wonder and admiration.

You must know, dear brothers and sisters, that good or bad does not depend on whether you respect conventions, but on the nature, the quality of what you bring to each other. Initiates are not preoccupied with whether the union of a man and a woman is legal or illegal, they are only interested in what good they will bring each other for their mutual edification, their respective evolutions. On that criterion they base their actions, because it is the essential. Initiates know how much humans have to work to perfect themselves before marriage, to purify and harmonize themselves, so that if they have a child, that child may be a manifestation of Heaven. Even without marriage in mind, Initiates work ceaselessly at purifying themselves, becoming enlightened in order to become divinities, without worrying about criticism against bachelors and spinsters! Actually they are not single, I will return later to this subject, but I will say now that many Initiates have made exchanges with the spirits of Nature, with beings who are utterly pure, such as sylphs, salamanders, undines, or devas ... delicate and marvellous exchanges which brought them indescribable happiness.

I will tell you something that happened to me. Several times, at night, I have been awakened by the presence of unreal creatures, diaphanous and extraordinarily beautiful. They surrounded me and looked at me, with such a look that I melted with love. They didn't touch me, they just stayed around me and looked at me, their power was all in their eyes. I have never seen such a look among humans. It seemed to come from very far, very high. And it lasted for hours ... I found out later that these creatures were devas, and I understood that they had come to visit me to show me that there existed in Nature a beauty greater than anything one could imagine. I was made to live in these states, so that I might know that they were possible. The devas opened up in me a new world. I cannot describe to you their absolute purity, their brilliant light, their radiant colors.... The Divine Mother who knows where my heart, my soul, and my ideal belong, sent them to me to teach me about love; they revealed many things to me about the true love which has no need for physical manifestation.

You say: "Yes, but that is only a world of illusion!" How do you know? And if it is illusion, I prefer these illusions to what you call reality, which is often ugly. It is preferable to live in a world of beauty where the things one learns and feels surpass the imagination. Nothing is more wonderful than to live in purity and be amazed at all the splendor of it without any physical desire for it. A single look can give you more happiness than all the rest. The one who can content himself with a look is near to perfection.

One day, when I was young, the Master Peter Deunov said to me: "For you, a glance is enough." At first I was surprised and didn't understand the meaning of his words, but I watched myself, and I have found it to be true, the Master had seen into the depths, the roots, the structure of my being, and in one sentence he summed it all up: all I need is one look. Later I learned how to use the look and I discovered several important laws; to be more precise, I discovered how to look in order to become sanctified, to be enchanted, to be enthralled and gladdened, to be made entirely happy with one look. For years I have worked on this, and it is something I have not yet told you about.

I have one absolute need, to be able to contemplate beauty, and I never want to be deprived of that. No matter who can tell me no matter what, and I will answer: "Do as you like, but leave me alone, I have a different path. You may be a saint or a great man according to tradition, and I admit it, but leave me alone; I have chosen another path that you don't know about . . . I have found my way." And without listening to a soul I will continue to contemplate. There is so much beauty on earth, it is too bad not to see it.

We shouldn't throw ourselves on beauty to eat it, but it is a crime not to find it and contemplate it. If humans make use of beauty to draw each other nearer to the precipice, it is not beauty's fault. It is they who are not well enough prepared, they stir up a fire within themselves that burns and smokes because of their impurity. Beauty is not there to make humans fall, but to bring them near to God, to project them all the way to Heaven. I would like to nourish myself with beauty, and I tell you: If God were not beautiful, if He were merely wise, omniscient and all-powerful, I wouldn't love Him. I am drawn by beauty, but pure beauty, spiritual beauty, not just any kind of beauty. I have another idea of beauty, often where others see something glorious, I see ugliness, and where they see nothing at all, I see a hidden splendour.

I was saying at the beginning of this talk that in the gatherings enjoyed by boys and girls, the boys unconsciously project rays into space, etheric particles which the girls receive, also unconsciously. The exchanges they make are thus on the etheric plane long before being on the physical plane, and that suffices to make them happy. But now, men must know that this is what occurs, and be conscious of these phenomena, and from now on project only the purest particles, capable of vivifying and healing humans. As for women, they should be careful to screen themselves from the dirty wastes of the psychic plane. Some are like sponges that absorb everything. There are a lot of rules to know, for if women are so often ill in these certain places, it is because they have received too many harmful influences against which they had no screen.

Since these etheric exchanges are realities, why not work toward realizing them divinely? Neither saints, nor prophets, nor the great Masters can keep the great laws of Nature from being accomplished. Even with very pure people, holy people, there are certain reactions, but they are conscious, and what they emanate is divine. The only preoccupation of the Initiate is to emanate divinity for the good of the whole world. You can't keep a spring from flowing or a river from running, but you can make sure the water is pure.

Sèvres, January 2, 1967

II

Little by little you will understand that when I enumerate the different degrees of love, it is always the same force, but with different manifestations and sensations. If you embrace a girl you feel a certain sensation, and if instead of embracing her you look at her with tenderness, you feel other sensations, less strong perhaps on the physical plane, but more intense and complete on the subtler planes, which bring you an indescribable joy. Yes, one smile, one look, can transport you with joy.

One day, in Paris, I was walking along the Boulevards, for a rest, because I had been meditating and working a great deal. The streets were crowded and I must have passed hundreds of people with whom I exchanged glances in passing. At one instant, a couple came towards me, a very young boy and a very young girl, and as she went by, the young girl threw me a look, a look so indescribable, so inexpressible, Heaven was in her eyes, it turned one upside down, it was blinding like a light, burning with love and beauty. Who was it that was speaking through this young girl? Because it was not she who looked at me that way, it was someone else through her, she was but the instrument. Often, there are people in the invisible world who wish to show you their love: it is perhaps your twin-soul who is not reincarnated, but who looks at you sometimes through the eyes of someone else. For days I was unable to forget the look of that young girl. You say: "But didn't you try to speak to her, to find her again?" No, there are things that I know that you don't know, and since it was not she who looked at me that way, if I had tried to find her, to have her look at me that way again, I would have been disappointed, her look could never again have expressed what a heavenly creature had sent me through her.

Believe me, dear brothers and sisters, if it happens to you that someone gives you such a look, a divine look, keep your impression, don't run after her to try to find the look again, for this person will be incapable of recreating it. You don't yet know about the delicate realm of the human soul I received a look that no girl on earth could have given me, it was so heavenly and divine. Of course I would have liked to go on forever receiving such a look, but it was too beautiful to happen often.

There is no person, no man, no woman, who can remain insensitive to such a heavenly look. If some are able to resist, it is because they are made of stone, even if they take themselves for Initiates, they are stones, and they are dead. A true Initiate is alive, he feels, he understands what is beautiful, he doesn't lose his head to beauty, but he feels it. To be pure is not to be made of stone. Many theories and mystical practices are twisted and deformed. One day these theories will have to be sorted out.

You must learn how to make exchanges with a look, but this look should carry no invitation, it should be friendly and without insistence.

Sèvres, January 1, 1970

Chapter XV

Wealth and Poverty

There exists a law that must be respected if we want to live intelligently and effectively. It is the law of polarity and it is based on the existence of two poles, one masculine and one feminine, one positive and one negative, one emissive and one receptive.

You all know, I am sure, the ancient custom of bringing gifts when calling upon a king, a prince, or a sage, a gift of fruit or cattle, or a priceless object. In India, when you visit your guru, you bring him a fruit, at least an orange or a mango, you never arrive empty-handed. Remember the three kings who came to see the Christ-child with their offerings of gold, incense and myrrh. They were kings and wise men themselves, but they followed the custom and arrived with their hands full of presents.

The masculine principle is represented by the one who moves, who is active, and the one who remains motionless, waiting for others to come to him, as for instance, the Christ-child in his crib, or the king on his throne, represents the feminine principle. The masculine principle is always the one to stir and go to the feminine principle and he bears with him an abundance of gifts. The masculine principle represents plenitude and the feminine principle represents the void, which the masculine principle fills with gifts. That is the meaning of this custom that dates back to the most ancient of times and that comes from a profound knowledge of the laws of life.

Plato deals with this subject in "The Banquet": "On the day that Aphrodite was born," says Socrates, "the gods were feasting, among them Resourceful, the son of Invention; and after dinner, seeing that a party was in progress, Poverty came to beg and stood at the door. Now Resourceful was drunk with nectar – wine, I may say, had not yet been discovered – and went out into the garden of Zeus, and was overcome by sleep. So Poverty, thinking to alleviate her wretched condition by bearing a child to Resourceful, lay with him and conceived Love." Love is, therefore, the result, the product, the child, of the two principles, plenitude (wealth) and the void (poverty). Plenitude brings wealth to the void. The void is an abyss, a chasm waiting to be filled, and plenitude goes forward and gives the void that which it desires.

Suppose you were going to visit someone. Since by doing so you play the role of the masculine principle, you mustn't arrive empty handed, you must bring with you a fruit, flowers, or the gift of a heart full of good thoughts and feelings. No matter what you bring, the important thing is not to be empty-handed. The feminine principle is not won with emptiness, that is by people who are static, passive and barren. The woman (material substance) is filled with wonder by someone who has everything in abundance. Take a man walking along the street, if he looks with half-closed, dull eyes at the beautiful girls passing by, do you think they will be enchanted and feel drawn to him? Possibly, there are women strange enough to fall in love with a man because of his moon-struck eyes. But usually, women prefer a man whose look is full of passion – they think: "There's a man!" A man means someone who is rich, abundant, powerful, active, dynamic, isn't that so? Yes, it is. It is written in the living book of Nature, but one must know how to read it, it needs to be studied.

If you always go to your friends with empty hands, actually or symbolically, they will end up not liking you, and they'll think: "But what is this? When he arrives he's empty, and he makes me feel empty too", and more and more they will leave you alone, they will be on their guard, until the day when the door to their souls and hearts is closed to you forever. This is the way stupid people lose their friends, by wanting always to profit by them. Don't go to see your friends if you are feeling empty, if you can't even take them a kind look, a warm smile, a few encouraging words, gifts that are alive. If you can understand the deep meaning of this custom of bringing gifts, you will greatly improve your way of behaving.

Let's go a little further. When you fill a bucket at a well or a spring, what do you do? You play the role of the masculine principle, moving about, walking towards the well while it remains motionless, but once you reach it, if you don't change the polarity you will not be able to fill your bucket. Therefore, for a minute, you identify yourself with the feminine principle, you become receptive and the bucket is filled. The well or spring, which is feminine since it does not move, is masculine as far as its flowing water is concerned, and you, who are at first masculine because you are in motion, become feminine because of the bucket you want filled. The water flows, it fills the bucket, and you go away satisfied. You say: "It's too simple, it's too obvious!" Yes, but wait for the conclusion to be drawn.

When you go near to God, how do you present yourself? He is there in His Heaven, He is waiting, representing the feminine principle, and you, you climb towards Him, you are the one to make the first move in order to seek Him out, and you represent, therefore, the masculine principle. You should be full of gifts at that moment, presents to put before Him, offerings of your heart and soul: "Lord, I offer Thee everything I have. . . ." Having given all, you are empty, and become the feminine principle. The Lord is the spring of water flowing forth, filling your heart and soul, and you become rich, enlightened, full of strength and power, and you return entirely happy. That is how to polarize yourself. You should first be active, dynamic, enterprising; you should think, concentrate and meditate. Then, when you succeed, like a bird on the wing that suddenly stops and floats motionless in the sky, you should cease all action, you should do absolutely nothing and you will be bathed in peace, in light, in silence. At that moment, you will feel that forces and blessings are pouring into you, and you are filled to overflowing with happiness.

Activity and passivity are two states of being that one must know how to use. The person who only knows activity is always tense and contracted, he can never reach an euphoric state of relaxation and peace, floating in a new world. You can't reach the second state without having gone through the first one, to stir the currents and set them in motion. And if you say: "Oh, it isn't worth it, I'm going to stay in the receptive state", well, you will be like the mediums who are so sensitive, so weak, that they fall to pieces ... because they don't know how to develop the masculine principle to protect themselves, to direct themselves consciously in the invisible world, instead of being exposed to all dangers, becoming the victims of all sorts of disorderly and anarchistic forces of Nature. To avoid being thus exploited, you should first manifest yourself as a man, active, energetic, dynamic, and then, armed with will power, you can permit yourself to let go, to remain passive, because the emanations and radiations that you have released will be harmonious and luminous, and will protect you from the hostile forces that would otherwise be devastating. You must know how to be both masculine and feminine, dear brothers and sisters, this is a most important exercise I have given you today. Never forget what I have just told you.

As for the full and the empty, I will add one more thing. You must realize that each one of your gestures is magic. Consequently, when you go to see someone in the morning, don't say good morning to him with an empty cup or basket or whatever, in your hand, because without wanting to, without knowing it, you are wishing him emptiness, poverty and failure for the whole day. You say: "But it doesn't matter, in the world people don't bother with things like that." If people are unconscious, it is no reason to imitate them. Let them do as they like, but here we are learning the laws of life, and we should practise being conscious, watching ourselves, and controlling everything we do. I beg you, put that in your heads, because I have been repeating it for years, and it's still as if I had never said anything. When you go calling on your friends in the morning, leave behind all empty receptacles, take with you something that is full, or fill your heart with good thoughts and good feelings, and wish your friends a good day. If you can learn to work with the positive forces of Nature, you will be loved, people will respect and admire you.

In certain countries, there are women sorcerers who know about the magic influence of a receptacle, either full or empty, and they purposely give an empty one to those they wish to harm, just as the person is leaving their house. By doing this they provoke serious, sometimes fatal accidents. You must never do it, even unconsciously, let alone purposely, for the penalty will be very severe.

One more thing: the friend you are going to see has the right to surround himself with objects that are empty. It is you who are going to him who must be able to fill whatever is empty. The person who makes the move, who goes towards the other person, should be positively polarized, he should arrive full. Someone will object: "But I'm not empty, I am full of rage, full of regrets, full of resentment, and am I to share that with my friend?" Of course there is plenitude and there is plenitude . . . we are referring here only to the most luminous and divine plenitude. You can also be full of manure and walk around with the kind of plenitude that will smell forever!

Le Bonfin, September, 1963

Complementary notes:

The void seeks plenty so as to be, at last, filled with happiness; plenty is attracted to the void so as to give of his abundance. One wonders whether the void will ever be filled, it is so vast! But still, plenty is also vast, they have been working this way since the beginning of time, and that is what makes the world go round.

As for the human soul, which is a virgin, she must be receptive, poor and humble, in order to attract the spirit of God and be fertilized by Him. Plenty repulses plenty, but humility is poor and rich at the same time, because it permits us to approach God. One must be humble towards God, to be filled with His plenitude; if you are full already and puffed up with pride, it is impossible. With human beings, it's different, if you want to help them, or keep yourself from being squashed by them, you must have plenitude. Therefore, we must be rich before men and poor before God.

Le Bonfin, July 23, 1963

Chapter XVI

To Love is the Work of
the Disciple

Yes, dear brothers and sisters, we must learn to love. "But that is what we do, you say, everybody does nothing else but love each other." I know, but perhaps this is not the way love should be understood. The great sanctuaries, the Mysteries of Initiation in the past, taught that only by loving can there be the improvement of self that leads to perfection, the final liberation. What do we have now? The contrary, for humans are debasing and limiting themselves with their understanding of love, and if they learn anything, it has to do with Hell: anguish, torment, and jealousy. It is true that they learn, but they learn everything on the negative side. We must return to the wisdom of the Initiates taught in the sanctuaries, which I remember for I was there . . . it would be impossible to deal with these issues without having had a thorough knowledge of them.

I also know that some of those who are here today started certain studies in the past which they did not finish. They left the Initiatic schools to live another kind of life and that is the reason for their present difficulties. To recover, they must again live according to the rules and laws that were given in the Temples. The knowledge of the Initiates will return to the surface only if we live according to their laws.

In the sanctuaries, the disciples were taught how to love the Creator, His creation, and all creatures. The Kabbalah gives us the same interpretation of God, the world and man. It is the same wisdom that was transmitted down through the ages ever since God first gave it to humans through the intermediary of the

Archangel Raziel. Such tremendous splendour could never have been conceived by humans without the great Initiates, who received their wisdom from the Archangels.

In the sanctuaries, therefore, the disciple was taught how to love. First of all, how to love God the Creator, because without this love there can be no progress, the contact with the higher realms is broken. If the current is cut off at the centre, your lamps won't light, your appliances can't work. So, the first thing the great hierophants told their disciples was the importance of preserving the connection with the centre, with the Lord. They told them how to prepare their inner mechanism, how to clean and purify their lamps, and afterwards, they were told how to connect them.

The quintessence of this instruction concerning love was given in the Gospels: "Thou shalt love the Lord thy God with all thy heart, and with all thy soul, and with all thy strength, and with all thy mind, and thy neighbour as thyself." Yes, but in between man and the Lord there is a whole world to love, with regions full of inhabitants. There is an entire science which explains how to communicate with the spirits of such and such a region, what words to pronounce, what gestures to make, what perfumes and what symbols to surround oneself with and what clothing to wear. Christianity has not given us many works that mention the hierarchy that exists in between human beings and the Lord, but when Jesus said: ". . . no man cometh unto the Father, but by me", he was expressing the teaching of the sanctuaries, presenting himself as an intermediary between the Lord and humans, as a medium, a transmitter.

Between Heaven and earth, there is an hierarchy, a living ladder, described in the Bible by the story of Jacob's dream. Jacob was told by the Lord to leave Mesopotamia, and during his journey he fell asleep on a rock. In a dream he saw a ladder rising all the way to Heaven and on this ladder were angels, ascending and descending. The ladder represents the angelic hierarchy as described in the Kabbalah, the uniting of Heaven and earth by the Christ. The word ladder is far from descriptive of the splendour and glory of this hierarchy, words can convey only a vague idea.

In the Initiations, the hierophant represented this ladder, he was the intermediary. The disciples learning about love took him as a point of departure for themselves, rising all the way to God. It is impersonal love that brings the greatest blessings. Unfortunately, humans who have no knowledge prefer to love neither the Lord nor their instructor, but to love some man or woman at the cost of ending with a catastrophe. This is what humans have learned: to reject every other form of love and to concentrate on some man or woman, thinking that he or she will give them something to hold onto, something to enjoy. But when the time comes to pay, what a disappointment there is! Don't let's talk about it! There is utter ruin because of having put all one's trust in someone untrustworthy. A person with no affinity for God is like a boat with a hole in the bottom, you load it with your valuable merchandise, and when the boat sinks you lose everything, and this is what happens all the time.

But when the disciple loves God above all, with all his heart and with all his soul, when he accepts his instructor, his Master, as a representative of the Lord, he is supported and enlightened by these two loves, by the fact that he is able to love unselfishly, disinterestedly, with a higher form of love, and when he comes to love a man or a woman, it will be entirely different, there will be no danger involved and no tragedy. His two higher forms of love will be there to protect him and guide him, they will give him an intuition, a clairvoyance and a wisdom that will also bring him plenitude, because love will be there in the three worlds. Without the first two, human love inevitably ends in disillusion, regret and ashes.

Yes, but humans are so blind and thick-headed they prefer to disagree with their Master and give their complete confidence to idiots. Just think of that! The Lord who is all powerful, omniscient, and their Master who is unceasingly connected with the Lord and whose one thought is to enlighten and help them ... Ah! those two are not to be trusted, they are the ones to oppose! Put your confidence in a drunk, a seducer, a thief, it's perfectly all right to give him your soul, your most precious treasure, but with a Master, be careful, beware! Yet he is the one who deserves to be loved, because he could never wrong anyone, never injure them. Even when you love him and say to him: "Here, take everything, I offer it all to you", he will answer: "Keep it for yourself, I have no need." If you should love a Master, it is not for his sake but for your own, it is you who will be able to advance because of your love. This love is for you, not for him, he has other things ... That is how you should think. When I say that you should have a Master and love him, I am speaking in the widest possible sense, a Master either on the physical plane or in the invisible world, a Master to enlighten us and help us, a Master who is noble and exalted and disinterested: a true servant of God.

You all have a need to love, but if you are able to give your love to the Lord and to your Master without running into danger, why go and give everything to some little idiot? Love anyone you wish, but let it be in third place, and then it will be your love for God and your Master that will guide you and you will be safe. Whereas now, you are not safe, night and day you tear your hair out, saying: "But I didn't know he (or she) would be like that!" You never will know, because you never ask the only people capable of enlightening you ... You are surprised? Well, I too am surprised, each day I am surprised at the way humans think and act.

Le Bonfin, August 16, 1970

Chapter XVII

Love in the Universe

People are looking for love, not a man or a woman. The proof is that men leave their wives (or wives their husbands) when they think they have found love elsewhere. It wasn't the woman who mattered, it was love. And if he doesn't find love with this one, he'll keep looking, a third time, a fourth time . . . it's love that counts, and not the man or the woman, otherwise they wouldn't ever leave each other. And suppose one had found love on a higher plane, one would no longer be looking for it since one would already possess it. It's because men and women haven't found it that they seek it through each other.

Actually, love exists everywhere in the universe for it is an element, an energy that is distributed throughout the entire cosmos, but humans aren't ready yet to absorb it with their eyes, ears, skin and brain. They confine it to certain little areas of their bodies where it is stored, and they look for it there and are happy with the few crumbs they receive, without realizing that love is distributed in profusion throughout the universe.

Love is everywhere, dear brothers and sisters, I learned that from a plant. As I told you, I get my information from stones and plants, insects and birds. One day, in Nice, I saw a plant that was suspended in the air, it hung in the air and subsisted on air and didn't need to bury its roots in the earth. I looked at it for a long time, and this is what it told me: "As long as I have succeeded in drawing the element I need – love – from the air, why bury myself in the earth as do the others? I have discovered a secret: I can draw everything I need from the air." There is an example for you, one that opens up new horizons, and proves that man also can find what he needs on other planes than the physical where he has always looked.

For the time being, let people look where they want. In the future, creatures will be more and more prepared to gather love in the atmosphere where it is as generously distributed as the dew. Because humans are like plants, some draw upon Mother Earth for their vitality, others draw from the realm of thought, the air; and others from the sun, from God Himself, since God is Love. Let us consider this example of the dew. Dew is vapourized water, everywhere in the atmosphere, which becomes visible only when it condenses itself in the morning on the plants. As all plants may not have a gardener to take care of them, Nature helps them by watering them at dawn with little drops that keep them alive. Nature has the job of watering the plants and every morning all over the earth, she pours out the dew. What is dew then, if not a kind of condensed love? And what is a ray of sun if not a kind of projected love? There you have it: everything in Nature is love.

Now let's take the example of breathing. Humans don't yet know how to breathe through the pores of their skin, and that is why their respiration is not complete and not correct. There are certain yogis who are able to breathe through their skin, thereby capturing all the energy and vital substance they need. This is an exercise you can do when you go to watch the sun rise: concentrate on absorbing the rays of the sun through your skin and then store them in your solar plexus. After a few months, or years, you will feel that the pores are like little mouths, little doors, which were always there but which you had never made the effort to use. Later, when man knows how to breathe through his skin, he will be able to diminish the amount of food and drink he consumes, because he will have learned to absorb a more subtle element.

Why must one always have a woman or a man in order to feel love? That is where limitations and unhappiness, difficulties and dependance come from. Love is life, it is absolutely indispensable. The Initiates themselves cannot live without love, but they seek, gather and draw it from all round them, and then distribute it on all sides. They are plunged in love all the time, they breathe love, they eat and contemplate love, they think about love all the time. This is why they have no need for women, they already have love, it is there boiling, exploding, filling them, it's marvellous, they are completely immersed in love. So why look elsewhere? Why would they wish to leave these wonderful feelings of plenitude in exchange for a few burning coals coming down on their heads? I am not opposed to love, on the contrary, but I merely say that we must learn to seize it, to find it everywhere. I find it everywhere, I look for it in every thing and everyone. Even without your knowing it, if you only knew how much love you send me!

You seek love, well and good, but you are always looking for it where the rest of the world looks for it, in those well-known, hereditary places which are supposed to be so fantastic. And I tell you that this is not the only place where love can be found, there is only a little part of it there, a few particles that are not really enough to quench the thirst of someone who is thirsty for an ocean. So you must go looking elsewhere as well. Like the dew, before it fell on the trees and flowers and grass, it was in space. Everything that exists on the physical plane can be found elsewhere in a greater state of purity. All the elements which are now materialized existed originally in the etheric state, and were condensed later, first as gas, then as water, and finally as earth. Why not seek them where they can be found in their subtlest state instead of always looking lower down where they are mixed with all kinds of impurities? In that way, by doing just that, the yogis of India discovered that with their breathing, they could draw from the prâna all the elements necessary for health. Medicine in the West has finally discovered that the most important elements for health are the most subtle, like vitamins and hormones.

You too must learn to look for love in the etheric regions, for that is where it is, not just a few drops of dew, but a whole ocean which you may drink to your heart's content for no one will stop you. If you were to walk on your neighbour's lawn because you had heard it was good for you to walk barefoot in the dew but you had no garden of your own, you would see what would be the result! Leave the little drops of dew alone, and go instead to the ocean ... there will be nothing to pay, it is simply there, huge, vast, infinite and inexhaustible. The only trouble is that it is far to go, but when you attain the heights, you will be flooded with plenitude.

Of course, there will be problems. If someone says: "Should I completely give up all exchanges with my wife in order to find the subtle form of love of which you speak?" I will answer: "My friend, I cannot answer your question just like that, it is too complicated. You and your wife must both agree, you must resolve the problem together, otherwise there will be a tragedy. And whose fault will it be? Mine. And who will be accused of breaking up marriages, of separating couples and families? Me." Because people don't know how to go about it, I am inevitably misunderstood. First of all, both the husband and wife must agree, and then they must go slowly, progressively, not ceasing all relations abruptly all at once. Very few people are ready to change their lives from one day to the next, and those who aren't ready will become ill. You must do as people do when they want to stop smoking. If someone smokes three packs of cigarettes a day and stops suddenly, he will suffer so much that two days later he will begin again. But if he stops progressively, his organism will adapt itself, and one day he will be able to give it up completely with no pain at all. There is a proper way to proceed in all things.

Don't accuse me later and say: "Since I came to the Teaching I am the most miserable man in the world." Were you happy before? I don't think so. In appearance maybe, because when you make no effort whatsoever, you appear calm, but during this time the impurities accumulate and the day comes when you have to suffer in one way or another. Whereas if you decide to purify yourself, naturally you are unhappy at first because you have started a revolution within, but afterwards there is a definite improvement. You have to understand. In the first case, in the guise of happiness and tranquility, it is actually your downfall that you are preparing. If you are not living an orderly life and you say: "I feel fine, I never felt better", you are mistaken, you are like the facade of a house whose beams are already eaten away by termites, nothing shows, but one day . . . so don't count on appearances. Since coming to the Teaching, you have probably suffered a few little inconveniences, but that is no reason to give up.

It is like people who decide to fast. As soon as they feel a little discomfort, headaches or palpitations etc., they are aghast, and give up fasting, thinking that they felt better as they were before. They don't realize that fasting is actually a diagnosis, it exposes the weak points of the organism, the places where the impurities have accumulated. You must not abandon your fast simply because of a little discomfort, but by the same token, you mustn't begin by fasting five or six days in a row. There too, you must give the organism time to adapt itself, you begin by fasting one day, and then two days, and the next time, three days. You must learn to be reasonable and you must learn the methods to use. If you go no further than appearances or if you don't know how to go about things, you will always be drawing the wrong conclusions.

Real joy is not to be found in a physical relationship. Take for example two young lovers. In the beginning they don't even kiss each other, but their lives are filled with such joy and inspiration! They get up in the morning and they go to bed at night with only one thought in mind, that the other one exists, that they will meet and talk to each other, they write poetry, they exchange a rose petal as though it were a talisman. But once they start to embrace, to sleep together, all the subtle side vanishes, they are no longer as happy, they don't think as much about one another, and the troubles begin, the time has come for settling the accounts. Before, they were in Paradise, why couldn't they have prolonged that state of bliss?

I know you are going to say that you can't go on forever taking homeopathic doses, a smile here, a word there, something more substantial is necessary. Well and good, but then don't be surprised and don't complain or reproach people with anything: eat your humble pie, suffer the results quietly, that's all. Since you don't want to live in poetry and light, since you must have something more substantial, I don't say no, but I say beware. I must still tell you about the other, higher degree of love . . . there are no words to describe it. . . . Everything is pallid beside the sublime love that doesn't depend on people or anything else, that you live uninterruptedly and which embraces all creatures. Yes, even with all their failings, they seem beautiful and delightful to you and you love them all.

                                                    Sèvres, January 11, 1970

Chapter XVIII

A Wider Concept of Marriage
I

Most humans are so limited in their love that except for their husbands and wives they forget the whole world, nothing else exists for them. As a result, they are lost in space, no one knows where. Humans are not used to understanding love in the greater sense, on a higher plane. Instead they diminish, impoverish and mutilate it. It is no longer a divine love that flows and waters all creatures. True love is one that embraces all creatures without growing roots closer to one than to the other, without limiting oneself or them. But what will the husband or the wife say of the one who decides to love the entire world? They will say that the Teaching encourages all sorts of abnormal behaviour, and instead of liberating themselves they will remain chained to their old ideas. Well, let them remain that way.

This Teaching is destined for those who wish to find a new life, having seen that the old way of life can neither protect nor save them, nor make them happy and free to move about in Heaven. The new life has already been found, it has been waiting for human beings for a long time, but they have not been ready to receive it. It was better to let them remain tied down somewhere because with these revelations they would do too much damage. As long as humans were in their primitive, coarse state, they couldn't be allowed freedom. Instead they were allowed a partner, to prevent them from causing too much trouble. This Teaching is not for everybody; it is only for those minds and souls who will not abuse their liberty.

Do not misunderstand me, I never said that you should not

marry and have children, but only that the husband and wife should have a larger conception of love and show a little less possessiveness and jealousy. The husband should rejoice at seeing his wife loved by everyone in the world, and the wife should be happy that her husband has such a great heart, but both should remain wise and pure. Marriage with its magnificent traditions and laws would then be safeguarded, and at the same time the husband and the wife, with the enlargement of their consciousness, would understand that up to then they had been too limited, and that they must enlarge their heart and love to include all creatures, without transgressing the laws of faithfulness and wisdom.

This is the real solution. We are not against marriage, we are not preaching against marriage in favour of living freely together, as they do in some countries. After a few experiences, they have all understood that the new way was not better than the old, and they have gone back to the traditional solution instead of finding a third solution, the right one. People are funny, they go from one extreme to the other, and never find the third solution. For each problem there exists a third solution which is always the one I seek . . . and on the subject of love, of the kind of behaviour to have in love, this also applies. As long as humans don't know about this solution, they will always be unsatisfied. Those who have decided to remain single feel that there is something missing and they are regretful at not having been married. As for those who are married, they are not happy either, and regret having done it. Neither one of them has found the right solution, the third. When humans find this third solution, whatever they do, married or not, they will always have happiness and plenitude.

Marriage should not be abolished. It has existed for so many millions of years that it has created an atavism and its abolition would entail all sorts of trouble. Suppose everyone were to say:

"No, the family isn't worth a thing, men and women should be allowed to do whatever they wish, let's have absolute liberty!" At the end of a short while, things would be so out of keeping with the established order from all points of view, physical, social, economic, and psychic, that there would be a return to the family as before. And then again they would have enough of the family, and so sensuality, decadence and libertinism of all kinds would take over until once again, exhausted and digusted, people would say: "No, no, the family was better" . . . and so on, ceaselessly, from one extreme to another, until the day they find a third solution. This third solution is not to be found in the family or in free love, it has to do with intelligence and it consists first of all of understanding that there exist other aspects of love, other purer ways of expressing it still more wonderfully, with husband and wife both trying to have the nobler and loftier idea of one another that allows them mutual freedom.

Most people cannot adopt this idea of love, too many of their ancient inclinations protest and fight against any change. But when two people marry who are truly evolved, then in advance, they leave each other this mutual liberty. Each one rejoices to be able to love all creatures, without rushing into anything with them; the wife understands the husband and the husband understands his wife, both raise themselves onto a higher plane and march together towards Heaven, becoming more and more enlightened and expansive, for they are living a true life, a life without limitations. That is the best solution. If you can't find either a wife or a husband who gives you this freedom but wants always to limit you, then it is best not to marry anyone, it is best to stay free to love whom you please without anyone to reproach you. If people are narrow and selfish and possessive to such a degree, it is not worth attaching oneself to them for a lifetime of trouble.

Le Bonfin, August 15, 1962

Chapter XIX

The Twin-Soul

Every human being has a twin-soul. When man leapt like a spark, a living flame, from the bosom of his Creator he was two in one, and these two parts complemented each other perfectly, each was the other's twin. These two halves became separated, they took different directions, and they have evolved separately. If they come to recognize each other at any point during their evolution, it is because each carries the image of the other in the depth of his being, each has put his seal on the other. Thus, each one carries the image of his twin-soul within. The image may be blurred but it is there. For this reason, everyone who comes on earth has a vague hope that he will meet somewhere a soul who will be everything he needs, and that with this soul he will find indescribable harmony and perfect fusion.

You all know this, each one of you has always believed that one day you would meet the beloved soul whose face you already know. But you carry the image buried so profoundly within you that you can't see it very clearly. Sometimes you see someone in the street and you think: "There it is, there it is!", as though there were a sudden fusion between the image you carry within you and the person you have just seen. Instantly your whole life changes and you do everything you can to find that person. When you find him, and talk with him, everything becomes marvellous, you can feel life circulating in you, you are able to make great progress in every direction. But then, after a period of intimacy, you discover it was not really this person you were seeking. You are disappointed and you leave him and begin your search again. A second time you think you have found your twin-soul in someone else. The same joy, the same inspiration surges within you, and once again, you are in love. But the same story repeats itself, and once again you perceive that it is not the being you were seeking.

"But then", you say, "the person wasn't my twin-soul?" Yes and no. It was the other half of yourself come from the other world, to pay you a visit through the means of another person. Usually only one half is incarnated, and the other waits his turn. What happened when we thought we had found our twin-soul? It is thinking about us in the other world, wishing the best for us, wanting our happiness, and thanks to the mysterious link which exists between us, it feels that we aspire towards a higher life, towards beauty. It therefore enters into another being and appears before us for a while. That is why for instance, a woman suddenly loves a man, thinking she has found her beloved again in him, because her twin-soul will have entered that person, for a short visit on earth, and will be sending messages of love through that person without his even being aware that he is thus inhabited. But usually the woman or the man, for these things apply to both sexes, needs to demonstrate love physically, which means that the twin-soul leaves, regretfully. Whereupon the man profits from this mistake she has made, taking him for her twin-soul, and the woman little by little realizes that the man is a liar, a thief and that her true love is gone. Perhaps he will come again in some other man . . .

This unhappy experience will repeat itself until men and women realize the sacred side of love. At that moment, the two halves will really find each other again, they will love each other, wrapped in light, swimming in happiness, without any wish to go further than the finer, delicate contact because they know this would break the ties that unite them to the primordial light. Before being able to reach this state of being, how many experiences will have been ruined, how many mistakes made, after which one says: "I have eaten, I have drunk my fill, I am gorged but miserable, never has possessing someone brought me true happiness!" It is criminal to have tried all the women in the world and never to have found illumination that lasted. But humans are used to being content with fleeting sparks of light.

Twin-souls complete each other, no other person in the world can so complete them. Thus, all the beings you have met since the beginning of your multiple incarnations, all the husbands and wives you've had, all the lovers or mistresses, have all left you, because they were not for you. Perhaps you were together for a short while, like a pot with a lid that doesn't match. Whereas two souls whom God has created together are absolutely made one for the other, and nothing can separate them; they have no fear of being separated. In a married couple, when one or the other is afraid that someone may rob him of his partner (and nothing can keep this from happening) it is because that partner was not really the beloved, not the true beloved, the twin-soul. A woman loves a man, he leaves her for another. A man loves a woman, she abandons him . . . but twin-souls, on the contrary, recognize each other with absolute certainty and can never leave one another.

A human being meets his twin-soul twelve times during his incarnations on earth. But, usually, this meeting brings about their deaths, because the conditions of our existence do not permit the realization of such a perfect love, such absolute love. Shakespeare's *Romeo and Juliet* deals with this subject, the meeting of twin-souls.

The day will come when twin-souls will bring children into the world differently from the way in which it is done now. They will surround themselves in light, they will project this light towards each other, and from the atmosphere thus created will be born currents of force which will envelop both of them. That which the man will then give to his wife will be absorbed by her in the greatest purity, and this purity will already have attracted the presence of a third being, their future child. Naturally, this child will have a perfect affinity with its mother and father. At the moment of the appearance of the spirit of their future child, the mother will receive in her solar-plexus a fluid that will envelop the child, and a few minutes later, the child will appear before his parents, exactly like them.

Of course, for the moment, humans are not yet able to produce children in this way, but the same phenomenon occurs in spirit seances. While the medium is in a trance, the clairvoyants can see a fluid, an emanation from the medium's solar-plexus, like a bright cloud which forms and makes it possible in a short time for a spirit to appear, a spirit that can even be photographed. The spirit who is incarnated by such a fluid cannot remain visible for very long because the fluid matter is very quickly reabsorbed by the medium. But in the future when humans give birth to children in this way, this matter will not be loaned, as it is now. It will be a gift, for ever. Obviously, for this to be possible one day, humans must work to attain absolute purity. The way we create children now is the animal way. Why is it done with the lights off, in darkness, in hiding? Because humans feel that this way is not worthy of the sons of God. God is neither so cruel, nor so ungenerous as not to have given humans some other method, but they have lost the secret, they have sunk too deeply into materialism.

Do not misunderstand me, it is not because you know for certain that your husband or wife is not your twin-soul that you should get rid of them. On the contrary, that is when you should realize that you are associated together in order to do a work together, and you must get along until the time when you are meant to go your separate ways.

Sèvres, February 28, 1942

Chapter XX

Everything Depends on
Your Point of View

All human drama comes from people not knowing how to consider each other. If you have a weakness for women, or men, and you fight against it and fight against it without ever being able to win, it is because you don't know how to fight. You rack yourself to pieces, all because you think you are strong enough to fight alone against the most powerful force that exists. What pride and what complacency! What arms do you have to fight with? Do not think you can confront forces about which you know nothing, without being bashed over the head and knocked down yourself.

In an Initiatic school, the disciple learns that in order to win, he must have the help of a force superior to himself as his ally, to fight his battles for him. For instance, if you want to resist seducing a pretty girl who is sitting temptingly in front of you, scantily dressed, and you count on your own strength, the more you fight against it, the more you will want to throw yourself at her. Whereas if you know how to look upon her as an aspect of the Divine Mother, not only will you not submit to temptation but you will soar to the heights, and remain for days in a poetic state of wonder. Think of each girl you meet as the Divine Mother who does you the honour of appearing before you in one of her manifestations, through a girl's face, a look, a smile . . . and thank her. Then instead of each one being a temptation for you, all the daughters of the Divine Mother will fill you with an indescribable sense of wonder and enrichment. Wherever you go, you will feel that the earth is peopled with creatures who are there to gladden your heart and bring you happiness . . .

Because they don't know how they should look at things, people are victims of their lusts and weaknesses, good for nothing but the hospital. Always fighting, fighting, no . . . you must know how to look, the whole secret is there. If you are a woman and you are tormented because you are constantly attracted by men, stop tormenting yourself; look at them as manifestations of the Heavenly Father, with His splendour, His intelligence, His strength, and then there will be no more temptation, no more danger, no yawning abyss. What hasn't been written on the subject! All because people didn't have the Initiatic knowledge that would have given them the correct way of seeing things.

Obviously, one can meet rather sad aspects of the Heavenly Father, drunks for instance, but it doesn't matter, say to yourself: "This one is a slightly deformed aspect, he has slipped a little, I'll leave him until later . . ." It isn't the fault of the Heavenly Father – He wanted to manifest through this man too, but the poor thing dragged Him into all the pubs and so the Heavenly Father abandoned him. He wanted to help him, but . . . and sometimes you come across an old shrew in a market who hurls insults at you, but she is also an aspect of the Divine Mother. Of course, poor old thing, she has left her state of grace, she would have done better to reflect on the glory of the Divine Mother, but she didn't know how, she didn't have the right conditions, and we must be sorry for her. Perhaps at heart she is good and kind, and if you asked her a favour she would do it where a young girl might refuse.

Start working with the idea that men and women are representatives of the Heavenly Father and the Divine Mother, and you will see how enhanced and enriched your life will become and how far you will advance! Even without knowing it, each man, because of the way he is built, because of his emanations, has the power to bring you closer to the Heavenly

Father. Through men, as through a door, go and seek the Heavenly Father. He is the only One who has everything, who is perfect. All the others are only one aspect of Him, and even if you combined all the men on earth, they couldn't represent exactly that which is the Heavenly Father, it would be so pale and inadequate in comparison. Take each man you meet as a bridge, an open door, that allows you to go all the way to the Heavenly Father and in that way, five minutes later, you have almost forgotten the other person, you have nothing else in your mind but your Heavenly Father. You no longer have any need to go and talk to the other person to get to know him, he was merely a stepping stone to bring you into contact with the Heavenly Father. Thank him for that, and take leave of him.

And if it is an adorable girl, look at her and let her fill you with appreciation for the Divine Mother. Who do you suppose gave this young girl her beauty? Herself? If so, she would have made herself twice as pretty, but the fact is that she cannot add one hair, nor shorten her nose by so much as one millimetre. What does she know about higher mathematics to be able to give her body such harmony and balance? Hers is a beauty she perhaps did nothing to merit. An Intelligence other than hers gave it to her, so why not bow down before such an Intelligence? You see, if you reason properly, you are compelled to seek out the author, the Creator, and say: "Divine Mother, how were you able to make something so perfect? What intelligence you must have to be able to make such radiant, pure and expressive forms. How much I admire you!" Speak to her for a moment, stay near to her for a while. During this time the girl will probably have left, but don't regret it because she is not what counts, she was useful in projecting you up to the Being from whom she received so many wonderful things. It isn't the girl who merits your love and consideration, nor certainly should you let yourself be upset or unhappy, ready to wreck your life because of her.

You must understand, dear brothers and sisters, that weaknesses, anomalies, seductions and failures come from not knowing how to look at things. We stop at the girl's or the boy's outward appearance, the physical body, and we go no further. How could you expect to escape? You will be seized by powerful forces, and that's it, you're finished, done for.

You have never thought this way, have you? And I, how do I know these things, these truths? And all the other truths that I have discovered, if you knew how many! But why tell them to you? No one is ready for them, and even what I just said will not be understood, nor believed, nor practised. If you have understood five percent, it is doing well. Those who come here don't know the value of what they are learning. It will enable them to transform their lives. They think it is too distant, too impossible, unrealizable.

I know it is difficult, but try just the same to understand, and from then on you will hold the key. If not, you will always be floundering around saying: "I can't do it, I can't do it . . ." And you never will be able to do it, because you will not have tried to understand what I am revealing to you now. Learn how to look at things. I realize that many families are in a tragic situation, first the husband is unfaithful, then the wife, and they live with lies. But if they knew how to consider each other, it would be different, both of them would be strong and happy.

Le Bonfin, July 31, 1965

Chapter XXI

A Wider Concept of
Marriage
II

I have never been one to reproach people for wanting to be
rich. I find this desire normal and I bow before it; it is right to
want wealth. I too, seek wealth. So, we understand each other,
you and I, we are both seeking wealth. Only the thing is, I
wonder whether once you have found it, you will be entirely
satisfied? You will never have much until you start searching for
the other kind of wealth, the one to which Christ referred when
he said: "Amass treasures ...". It is God Himself who gave
humans the instinct to amass treasures. Only the difference is that
instead of seeking these treasures above, they look for them
below.

And you, dear brothers and sisters, if you looked for riches
within (within and above are the same thing), once you found
them, you would be completely satisfied, rich, happy and free.
Whereas with the other kind, it's not so sure. One must therefore
tell humans: if you want wealth, that's fine, marvellous, but try to
lift this desire onto a higher plane. Furthermore, in sexual love
... who put this tendency in humans to seek out a woman or a
man? It was also the Lord. Unfortunately, we seek them only on
the physical plane, and even when we find them we are not
happy.

All humans want to find love, the wish is natural and
legitimate, but they should ask themselves if it is enough to look
for love only in one place, or if they should not be looking higher
up. Yes, put the question this way and you will find the solution

to many of your problems, you will avoid untold grief and woe.
There is no harm in looking for love on the physical plane, but
only as a point of departure, on the way to the real love which is
higher up, always higher and higher. I know that you are looking
for your twin-soul; everyone is looking for his twin-soul except
me. Why? Because I have found her. Now you are wondering
which one of the young girls here . . . well no, not here. My twin-
soul includes all the women on earth. With one woman only,
there is nothing but trouble, but with all women, one is saved!
Therefore, all the women on earth are my twin-soul. That is how
I see the problem. Above all women is one Woman. Above,
there is only one man, one woman, Adam Kadmon and his
Beloved, who are reflected here on earth in a multitude of men
and women. But actually there is only one woman and it is
precisely this woman who is my twin-soul. You say: "Am I
included?" Of course, my twin-soul includes the whole world.

You may think you have found your twin-soul, but it is not yet
more than its reflection coming from a woman or a man.
The proof is in the fact that all women, everywhere on earth,
reflect only a little bit of the beauty of the cosmic Woman, one
feature, a nuance; in one it will be the skin, in another, the eyes
or hair. . . . This beauty that we see in women, is all a part of the
beauty of a single woman, cosmic Woman, the Divine Mother
who is splendour itself. If you seek perfect beauty, rise up to the
heights where you will find the Divine Mother in all her
perfection, with all the virtues. And all the men on earth also
reflect something higher, the beauty and power of the Heavenly
Father, some more, some less. By loving one man or one woman,
you can never be satisfied, never really happy, because they won't
have total beauty.

Of course what I am saying shouldn't lead you to neglect all
humans for the sake of loving only the Heavenly Father and the
Divine Mother. In the family, for instance, the father is the
symbol of the Heavenly Father, that's why you should love him
and think of him as a way of bringing you all the way to Him.

And if you have a teacher, a Master, he too represents the Heavenly Father, and by linking yourself to him, you will be able to go more easily towards the Deity. But don't have any illusions: he can bring you to the Heavenly Father, but he himself is not the Heavenly Father. Thus, everything is in the way you consider these things. Beings such as Jesus and Buddha, can help us to go rapidly to the Heavenly Father because they fill this role, they play the part, they are more fitting for the part than the father of a family for example, because how many fathers are that good? From the symbolic point of view, there is nothing to say, he may be a drunk, and illiterate, but since he is the father of the family, he represents the Heavenly Father. And the mother, even if she is a shrew, an untamed shrew, it doesn't matter, she represents, however inadequately, the Divine Mother.

When the true philosophy arrives, don't think there will be no more love, no more marriage, on the contrary, that is the time when we will begin to love each other as we should, because we will know how to judge things. Do you think it makes sense to take some young fool for the moon and the stars and discard the rest of the world because of him? The need to love is a need that is normal and natural, but we must learn how to centre this love, on whom to bestow it and in what way. Marry and have children, be faithful to your husband, but face the fact that husband and children can give you only what they have to give.

I only know one path, I have studied only one subject: it is the power of love. We must know how to love, it is love that will bring us to the summit, nothing else. Hysteria, nerves, depressions, always come from a wrong idea of love, love wrongly directed, wrongly controlled, love wrongly interpreted. Each time, we must take love and raise it to a higher region, higher and always higher until it comes into the regions of the Heavenly Father and the Divine Mother.

Sèvres, December 31, 1963

III

I was speaking to you this morning about the great universal Soul, the Divine Mother, of whom all women are but a reflection. I didn't say that men should only love the Divine Mother and always look for the Divine Mother across other women, to the exclusion of marriage. There are not many who are capable of this. Most men can love only one woman at a time. Well and good, it is better this way, but why not try to love all women through her? You will say that if you told your wife: "Darling, I love all the women in the world through you," it would not be such a good idea. Yes, but if women were also taught to see all men through their husband, everything would fall into place. I know very well that with our narrow culture it would be difficult, but with instruction and education, in time it will come. Men and women will stop being so jealous, so limited and so personal. Furthermore, why is man jealous? Because he is ignorant, and I will prove it to you. When a husband loves his wife, it is only because of his ignorance that he can be so confident of her, because if he knew what was going on in her head, how many people come and go and help themselves! A wife is also in communication with the entities of the earth, water and air, and when she looks at the sun, how many angels come down to her and kiss her and bring her gifts? The husband, poor simpleton, says nothing about it because he sees nothing. It is only on the physical plane that he reaches for his gun if someone touches her. And the same thing is true for him, to a lesser degree perhaps, because man is less active psychically than woman and he is not as much affected by the invisible world.

I know this philosophy will not take up much space in the human mind, because humans have been working for hundreds and thousands of years to establish a certain order, and if you ask them to break this order, to change their traditions, you will be sure to run into danger. But you should know, dear brothers and sisters, if you wish to be free, happy, and useful, if you wish to live in the infinite, try to find beauty, all the beauty of all women in the divine Woman. Make an image for yourself of a woman so beautiful, so expressive, the epitome of everything beautiful in colours, in music, in perfumes, in softness and gentleness, in life . . . Of course, this will not prevent the disciples, men or women, from loving other men and women, but as their hearts and souls will be full of their love and appreciation and admiration for a perfect and celestial being, they will be protected from all temptation and its consequences. And if one day they decide to get married despite everything, with this same philosophy of Heaven always in mind, I am absolutely sure they will be much freer, they will have peace and light, and joy.

If you are devoted exclusively to one man, obviously he will be proud and happy to see that you are his slave, that you are nothing without him, but for you, I am not so sure it means happiness. And if a man is completely devoted to one woman, if he is her slave, the woman's vanity will be gratified, but is it good for him? For thousands of years, men and women have been trying to put each other in chains in order to satisfy their vanity, unrealistic as it may seem and contrary to all common sense, it makes no difference, they still have to satisfy themselves, satisfy their personalities, never mind about reality or common sense. And men become unfeeling brutes and so do women. But when they see this question in a new light, this order of things will change. You say: "But it means the end of the family, it will be chaos and disorder and anarchy!" No, because this love is the real love, this way of loving doesn't end, it doesn't ever come to grief, it makes them both grow and flourish, it projects them all the way to God. Both understand each other, they can get along, they soar together and work together, they are partners, with no jealousy between them, and they are an influence for good on the entire world.

Sèvres, December 31, 1963

Chapter XXII

Analysis and Synthesis

The Maître reads the thought for the day:
"With analysis you descend into matter and with synthesis you rise towards the spirit. As we go higher we lose sight of details, the whole becomes apparent, and we perceive a greater quantity of facts and objects. The higher we go, the more we have to make a synthesis. Thanks to synthesis, we grasp the meaning of unity, we see that all things are connected, which means that we are on the road to knowledge. Knowledge comes from looking at everything from the highest point possible, in order to have the widest view and to be able to see everything. Along with this knowledge come power, health, and joy, which cannot be gained unless there is unification of energy, a convergence of all the energies towards a single point, the point that is beyond all possible divergence."

This way of understanding analysis and synthesis will no doubt surprise you, for it is not the way they are usually defined. It is a fact, however, that analysis is the descent into matter, for in order to analyse, you must get a close view of things, and separate them in order to study them. It is this separation of the elements that gradually leads to death. Death is nothing more than complete analysis, whereas birth, on the contrary, is a synthesis, elements come together to form a unity and a child is born! The birth of a child is the synthesis of all the energies and all the particles.

Synthesis is life, analysis is death. That is why the tendency today towards analysis is so dangerous. All specialists are analysts, for instance. Their efforts are devoted to one object only, a single organ, one component, they neglect the rest – the situation as a whole, the whole man, the whole universe. They are heading towards death. Of course some forms of specialization are necessary, specialists are needed, but by dint of analysing, one loses sight of the entire picture.

Scientists are working more and more in the field of analysis, discovering ever more minute particles of matter, always splitting up and breaking down, dismembering, disintegrating, smashing. And this is how science tries to know the human being also, pulling him apart to study separate pieces. The trend toward separation that has been so stressed and magnified by scientists has brought about changes in our moral and spiritual life, and everyone now wants to be isolated, separate from others – hostility, prejudice and war are the results of analysis. Patriotism, for instance, is nothing but a manifestation by nations of this philosophy of universal isolation. Everyone is for analysis, division, separation, everybody is split up, severed. Even families have become such analysts they can't stand things any longer, they are forever splitting hairs, the mother with the father, the parents with the children. . . . They haven't understood that we need to study synthesis, because synthesis is love, mutual understanding, agreement.

They all rush to analyse, they enjoy analysing, studying microbes and illnesses. . . . If they were healthy, if there was synthesis in their lives there would be no need for analysis. Why so much analysis? Analysis of the blood, analysis of the urine and who knows what. . . . We've had so much analysing we can't get along without it. Think about synthesizing and you won't need analysis! You may not know about your urine, but no matter, you will be healthy. Analysis is everywhere now, even Brittany is for analysis, and Corsica also is for analysis. Everyone is an analyst and before we know it France will be analysed into pieces! Here we are in favour of synthesis, with all countries becoming one country, with life circulating freely. Synthesis means life, life eternal, immortality. Very few are going to understand what I am saying, I know, because their minds have been distorted by false facts prevalent in papers, books and films. . . . It is the fashion to uproot and tear down, to cut up and to remove.

I will go even further and say that humans who choose one woman or one man only, are analysts. They are asking for trouble, and sorrow and grief will fall on their heads. They enjoy one person, they don't want to know more than one person, they have eliminated everyone else. In the Great Universal White Brotherhood we teach humans to be synthesists because our aim is to gather together the whole world, to love the whole world, not only one person who will turn your life into a series of problems. You are angry, of course, and you say: "Oh, how can he talk this way about love and marriage, he is being disparaging about things that are sacred." No, I am explaining how things are from a philosophical point of view. Now, if you would prefer something else, that is your affair, I don't interfere with your affairs, I simply explain things, innocently and candidly, and you have nothing to say about it.

Love is synthesis. When you love someone, you want to be close to them, to unite with them. We may learn through analysis, but with synthesis, we feel and live; with analysis there is not much to feel, whereas with synthesis we may learn nothing at all, but we feel, we expand, we live through ecstasies and rapture. If humans are less and less capable of divine and heavenly experiences, it is because they are too steeped in analysis. When you meet someone, you start right away to analyse him: his nose, his mouth, his gestures . . . his qualities and faults, his profession, how much money he makes. . . . Whereas if you love him, you don't care about any of that, you love him as he is, you are aware of his whole being, you vibrate in unison with him, it is a synthesis. If you become irritated with him, immediately analysis takes over, and you cut him in pieces. Then again, when you rediscover your love for him, you forgive him because you see the whole picture and you forget the details. Synthesis doesn't dwell on little things, contrary to analysis, which not only dwells on them, but enlarges them to such an extent that for the sake of a flea, the bedcover is burned, as they say. Someone will be ruined because of some little weakness that amounts to nothing. He may be a son of God, but no matter, that is overlooked, it is the weaknesses they look for.

Towards the end of the passage I just read it says: "Thanks to this synthesis we grasp the meaning of unity . . . we are on the road to knowledge. Knowledge comes from looking at everything from the highest point possible, to have the widest view . . ." Yes, true knowledge is to be found in synthesis. The knowledge you obtain with analysis is not true knowledge, it is only superficial knowledge, and it is not complete. You can't learn much from studying each element separately. To find out something really important, you must adjust the elements so that they produce something they didn't have before, when they were separate, and that something is life. True knowledge is to be found in life itself. When you unite the elements, something new happens and this new thing is life. You can know all about the properties of each element, but as long as you haven't life, you have no real knowledge. The true knowledge that permits you to see the whole picture clearly is the knowledge of unity. Unity is the most important thing, because it allows you to converge all the forces and energies towards one point and then they are at peace, in harmony; they work together and you become very powerful. This unity belongs to the spirit.

If humans have not this philosophy, it is because they have taken the path towards materialism. This is fine, magnificent, they will make all kinds of discoveries and acquisitions, but if they continue, they will go so far from the unity of spirit which is the only thing that maintains harmony between people, they will become so hostile and so selfish, that they will end up destroying themselves. If they decide on the other hand to climb towards spirit, towards unity, love and synthesis, then it will be possible for the Great Universal White Brotherhood to exist throughout the world. Everyone will want to be together, to rejoice together, to study together. This is synthesis, not to be stuck together the way the elements are stuck together in objects, no, but to realize together the Kingdom of God on earth, the Golden Age.

By choosing materialism humans are choosing the way of annihilation. They think they will be free, but instead they are burying themselves. They don't want to listen to Initiates, they feel they know everything, but the day will come when they will be completely crushed under their own load, this matter which they won't let go of and which they love so much. If one could work with matter while adopting the point of view of the spirit, one could do much more with it; for it would have to obey superior strength. The other way it doesn't obey at all, it says: "Aha, I've got him tied hand and foot, he does everything I want, satisfies my every whim. This is great, I'm going to take advantage and make him my slave." Matter, you see, is not afraid of man. Since man rejects everything to do with the spirit, he will have to accept the consequences because never in this way has anyone succeeded in liberating himself from matter ... instead he is bound tighter and tighter, imprisoned, fettered, and hampered, and it ends very badly for him.

Here, we have the Grande Fraternité Blanche Universelle, the Great Universal White Brotherhood, the Teaching that can bring you eternal life, believe me, but you need to change your way of thinking and living. For years I have been showing you how. Those who are here for the first time should study and practise, for it is wrong to imagine that one can know all there is to know in one day, and that instantly everything will adjust itself. A student went to Germany to see a famous professor of Natural Science. He asked him: "Sir, I would like to study Natural Science, but much more rapidly than the other students, is that possible?" – "Yes, it is possible," answered the professor, "if you observe Nature, you will see that when it wishes to make a pumpkin, a few months will suffice, but it requires a century to make an oak. Which do you wish to be, a pumpkin or an oak? . . ." I ask you also which you wish to be, pumpkin or oak?

Le Bonfin, August 25, 1974

Chapter XXIII

Like the Sun,
Love Brings Order to Life
I

To be organized means to be alive, because it is life that organizes things. Let water take its course and it will organize the sand and stones in its path; let life circulate, the current of life, and it organizes everything. When life ceases to circulate, everything stops. In winter, the sun doesn't shine and nothing grows. But as soon as spring arrives with its light and warmth, life circulates, and the seeds and plantings all begin to stir and sprout. What about man? Well, as long as the spiritual sun doesn't shine within him, the divine life can't flow and the seeds within him will not germinate.

Everybody, even children, know that the sun makes the seeds grow, but they haven't really understood, because if they had, they would seek the spiritual sun, bask more and more in its rays of love and wisdom, and bring to fruition the virtues and talents and abilities that God gave them. We have need of the spiritual sun as well as the physical sun, and thanks to this sun, the rivers flow, the birds sing and the trees flower and give fruit.

There is much to be said about the word "organization". Humans always think of organization as belonging to the mechanical world, but that is not all. It is love that organizes. When there is love among humans, there is no need for organization, everything organizes itself, each one knows what he should do and everything works perfectly. Take away love, and you have to threaten and censure and even then nothing works. If there is love in a family, everything works of itself, but take away love and even if you send in people with machine guns and force, nothing will work. When real love invades the world, there will be no need for laws or rules, everyone will know exactly what to do and they will do it in harmony with each other. Love is the only thing that organizes everything and makes things grow and flourish. Give a family love, or give society love, and you won't need to say: "Do this, do that, and if you don't, beware!" Everyone does it with pleasure, without any laws. Where there is love there is no need for law.

Law was invented the day love disappeared from mankind. There was a time when people were capable of loving each other and remaining faithful, and the institution of marriage didn't exist. Marriage was invented because humans forgot how to love each other: they got married for no good reason, without really knowing why and then separated, so, to restrain them, they had to invent laws, the sacraments, etc. Where there is love, does one need a document or a contract, is there a need for the Registrar or the clergy? Even with all the documents and the mayor and the clergy, you can't keep couples from divorcing. When love is there, nothing is needed to make it last forever, not even the priest's blessing, because God has already given his blessing. God is a part of the love of people who really love each other, and that is the blessing, their love is the blessing.

I am not against marriage, I am not against the clergy's blessings. I am explaining that if love is missing, these are human institutions which can never do much about anything. This doesn't mean one shouldn't be married in church, or go to the Town Hall to legalize the situation. I am just saying that those who love each other are already married by Nature, even if they don't know it. Whereas those who don't love each other, even if they are married by the priest and married by the mayor, are not married by Nature.

Sèvres, May 8, 1966

II

Human understanding is at such a low ebb that everyone has become mortified. For humans, the earth and sun are not alive, let alone intelligent. They themselves are the only intelligent ones! How could an intelligence that existed nowhere else be able to find its way into the human brain? If man has fabricated his own intelligence, one feels prompted to ask: "Well then, old man, why are you so stupid and so limited? Since you are the author of your own intelligence, why didn't you invent something a bit better or give yourself a bit more?" Logically, we must admit that this intelligence which manifests itself in the human brain exists everywhere else as well and it is humans in their ignorance who impede their own progress, denying that there is life everywhere and prefering to mortify everything.

The truth is that everything is intelligent, everything is divine, even stones and metals, which are the ones with the least amount of life on the huge ladder of life that rises all the way to the Lord. And the task of the Initiates is just that, to bring humans to feel the life of the universe and communicate with it in its purest and most intense aspect. It is for this reason that I am bringing you to the sun, and because of the sun, if you know how to look at him, think about him, and love him, you will move towards a higher degree of life, you will be able to create another current in your cells and organs which will function differently, emanating something so subtle and fine that little by little it will attract towards you the love of the whole world. It is life that humans seek. Yes, true but terrible. You take a woman who adores her husband, he means everything to her, she admires him and loves him for the way he looks, his strength, his intelligence . . . and one day, he dies. What does she do? Does she stay with him? No, she says: "Bury him!" The moment life leaves, she leaves him, for you can't stay with something that has no life. We don't love corpses.

People are becoming more and more like corpses. There they are, cold and loveless, nothing very remarkable emanates from them, and they think that this is the way to succeed, poor things! Well no, let them first get into the habit of being alive! And you are only alive if you emanate love. It's so easy to practice! For instance, when no one is looking, lift your right hand high and project all your love to the whole universe, to the stars, to the angels and archangels, saying: "I love you, I love you, I want to be in harmony with you!" And in this way you form the habit of always emanating something vibrant and intense, you become a living source, a source of love. Humans think they are safer behind a grim face with no expression, reflecting nothing alive, no kindness. They don't realize how dangerous this is. Just because some idiot somewhere decided to take a closed, frozen attitude, and others thought they were being clever by imitating him, now everyone wants to look that way, as though it were the height of evolution. Well no, first the poor idiots should learn to emanate love, to be alive, so that everything in their face and their glance is alive. Sometimes, I look at someone's eyes, and nothing vibrates, there is no answering gleam, the eyes are like stones. I dislike looking at eyes like that, and I have to turn my head aside. They are dead, the eyes are dead. When will people understand that we love life, not death?

We must form the habit of vibrating, night and day, thereby giving to all creatures in Heaven and earth something of ourselves, penetrating them with our love, like the Lord. That is what the Lord does. He is constantly infiltrating Himself into all creatures in order to give them life, to infuse them with His qualities. Yes, that is what God does, that is His work: to penetrate all creation with His love which is infinite, and thanks to this love, the particles, the currents, all harmonize with each other of their own accord. The proof is that if someone has a pain in their solar plexus, or a headache, and you place your hand on the painful spot with much love, all the particles that were agitating around in all directions hurry to take their places again because of the love you are giving them, whilst all the harmful particles that had slipped in, leave. If your love is strong enough, very strong and very powerful, you will have results, otherwise it is useless to try.

If you wish to be alive, love! "Oh! I see", you say. "We must go and find a man or a woman to love!" No, no, not that way, that way you will be inviting death, the death of the spirit. If you throw away this quintessence that belongs in the brain, uselessly, stupidly, you will weaken and coarsen yourselves. And those who inhibit themselves are no better off, they fall ill. The only solution is to project your love towards Heaven, for it to be alive and not stagnant, for it to circulate, and not break all the dams and start a flood, an inundation. That is the reason for loving, loving day and night, thinking about sending your love to all creatures who need love. When I come into the hall and greet you, I send you my love, all my love, and even if you are not aware of it, I am happy, I am glad because of it. Why have you not understood the importance of saluting each other with love? We should greet each other in such a way that the angels and archangels watching us say: "How marvellous! What a shining light! Let's go and join those people greeting each other with so much love!"

People meet and greet each other and then separate, and there is no love between them. Married couples kiss each other: "Goodbye dear, goodbye dear . . ." but their kiss is empty. They kiss out of habit, because it is customary, and this is very wrong. Why kiss at all under those conditions? You must put something into a kiss so as to imbue the person receiving it with life, to revive and invigorate him. Humans don't know what a kiss means, nor how they should kiss each other. It is when a man is miserable and unhappy that he kisses his beloved to comfort and console himself, and his kisses hold all his grief and discouragement, so that the poor girl who swallows it all soon falls ill. Men and women are forever making exchanges with each other, but what exchanges? God only knows ... or rather the devils only know. It's not forbidden to kiss, on the contrary, but you must know how and when, so that your kiss will transmit eternal life.

So, dear brothers and sisters, if I tell you that you don't even know how to kiss the people you love, you will be horrified because according to you, everything you do is perfect, ideal. It is only the Initiates who can see how far off you are.

The most important thing is life, or love, because life and love are one and the same. That is why you must get out of your static lives, your prosaic and ordinary little lives, and keep the highest ideal before you: to emanate the divine life, the divine love. Never say: "I am not able to, I am not evolved enough, I give up." Even though your ideal is unrealizable, inaccessible, hold on to it. It is just because it is inaccessible that it is marvellous. Accessible goals are not very worthy ones ... the entire world clings to things that are easy to obtain, but I, twisted since birth, threw myself into something that I knew ahead of time would never be realized, because it was too great, too lofty, too idealistic. Well yes, but that is what stimulates me, it fills me with enthusiasm and poetry. If I were to cling to easier things, I would lose my enthusiasm. Psychology hasn't delved enough into this aspect. You will say that it has nothing to do with psychology, but it has, it is the true psychology. Never ask yourself if you are capable or incapable, work on emanating the divine life, the divine love.

Le Bonfin, July 14, 1975

Chapter XXIV

Mother Love

Before a young girl marries and has children, perhaps she puts the love of God in first place. She may love purity and wisdom, she may think, meditate and pray, and really wish to be an example to others. But once married, and with a child . . . she puts her married life, the life of the child and the family in first place and abandons the rest. I would like to analyse this attitude.

Everybody agrees with this mother, they think it absolutely right and normal that she give up her spiritual life for the sake of the child. She is the mother, the child is hers, all the other mothers and fathers will approve. But I don't agree with this point of view, for if this mother puts everything else aside for the child, if nothing is more important to her than her child, she will break all divine laws and she will even quarrel with the Lord and accuse him of cruelty and unfairness if anything should happen to the child. Everyone thinks this kind of love is marvellous except me. To me it is clear that if she loves her child and not all children, if she can put aside God, it is simply because she loves the child for herself and is thinking of herself and not of him. She abandons the Deity and the light in order to consecrate herself entirely to the child, but by so doing she keeps him from all that is divine, from the source of life, from the immensity that the child will perhaps never know or be able to benefit from. Because of her stupid love she takes him away from the place where he belongs, where he could become immortal. Thinking she is caring for him, she leads him nearer to Hell, by keeping him away from Heaven, the Source of light and harmony.

So you see, this is a misunderstanding that has been in

existence for thousands of years. The mother who loves her child should never separate him from Heaven where all living creatures blossom. If she leaves God behind in order to think only about her child, her thinking will no longer contain divine elements and there will be no life in the nourishment she gives him.

A mother should never take care of her child without first going close to God, without first finding life for him by connecting herself with God. But, stupidly, she thinks that if she is not there to take care of him all the time he will die. On the contrary, he will be revived. Even if he were to die while she is with God, when she returns she will be able to revive him! But if she stays with the child without ever going close to God, and he should happen to die, never will she be able to revive him. You will say it is very difficult to make sense out of what I am saying. No, if in the midst of her occupations, the mother does not seek God, does not seek that which is alive and luminous, she will not be able to radiate the shining particles which would make him an exceptional being. Her love will be ordinary, and it will create an ordinary child. He will be alive, he will be clothed, but he will be a child like all the others, because he will have received his training far from the presence of God. Whereas the mother who knows the Initiatic science will go near to God and say: "Lord, I come to you seeking the light, love, health and beauty I need for my child . . ." And when she returns, she will give him elements that ordinary mothers know nothing about. They have no time! They have time, but the selfishness of their love doesn't allow for such a philosophy. That is why this earth will be forever populated with nothing but ordinary children, because their mothers are ignorant.

As long as mothers and fathers are too attached to their families to leave them and seek instruction, they will never be able to transform the family nor make it happy, for you cannot transform the members of your family by remaining close to them. I don't mean leaving them physically, but leaving them mentally, in order to replace a mistaken way of loving and understanding them. Once married, once there are children, it is all over, women become subjugated, they are slaves: "Mother hens" as they say, and the world is full of hens!

You say: "But this is a crusade against our children!" Not at all, maybe I love your children more than you do, it is debatable. If there is someone who loves your children, it is I, I am perhaps the only one who does. You, you don't really love them. Once a boy demanded money from his mother to do a lot of crazy things, and he threatened to kill himself if she didn't give it to him. So the mother replied: "Go ahead, my child, go and kill yourself, we don't need people like you on earth. I wanted to make you into something exceptionally fine and noble, but you prefer to behave like a criminal, so go ahead and commit suicide, it would be better that way. I will thank Heaven when you are dead." Well, because of her daring, for the first time in his life the son stopped and listened and subsequently turned into a wonderful person. Years later he said: "It was my mother who saved me." If his mother had torn her hair out and said: "O my poor boy, don't do that, here's the money," she would have turned him into a brute, and that is what most parents do: because of their blind goodness, their spinelessness and lack of character, they turn their children into inhuman wretches. And they say: "But we love them." They justify their stupidity, their inability to teach or use psychology by saying: "We love them." That's what passes for love! Instead of saying: "How weak and stupid we are!" they say: "We love them" I alone do not believe it. Behind those words, "We love them", I hear something else: "We are idiots".

A mother shouldn't set aside Heaven to devote herself to her child. She should take the child with her to Heaven, and she should tell him when he is still in his cradle, before he is able to understand: "I am taking you with me to Heaven, up to the light, to where harmony reigns." And the child's soul will listen and understand. That is how the mother should begin to train him when he is still very young, otherwise the child will be ordinary, maybe even a criminal. "What? A criminal? My child is an angel!" We will see whether he grows up to be an angel. In a few years, if you are stupid, you'll see whether he's an angel! But if you are intelligent, yes, he'll be an angel, more than an angel, a divinity. There, it is clear, it is mathematical. Now, what you think about this yourself is another question; what I think is more important. Why not learn to think as I do for Heaven's sake? Be daring!

Abraham loved Isaac, but he accepted to sacrifice him. God wished to see whether Abraham loved Him more than he loved his son. We are always asked this question, whether we love our children more than we love God, but fathers and mothers never suspect that there might be such a question. God wanted to test Abraham and so He asked him to offer his son in sacrifice. You say: "What? The Lord was not clairvoyant enough to know that Abraham loved Him, He needed proof?" No, the Lord knew in advance what Abraham would do, He read his heart, his thoughts, but it was Abraham who didn't know which he loved best, and it was necessary that he should. It was for Abraham's sake that God put him through this trial, not for His sake, and that is why God tests us, to teach us to know ourselves. We don't know how resistant we are, nor how intelligent, strong, good, generous, weak or stupid. We imagine all kinds of things: "I am a genius, I am this, I am that," but when faced with a little test we capitulate, we don't understand why. And Abraham found that he loved the Lord more than anything else. He knew that since God had given him his son, God could also take him away.

Why don't mothers think this way? They want to save their child even after abandoning the Lord, and they think the child will be safe under their protection. But what protection can they give when they are not even protected themselves, since they have turned their back on the great Protector? What pride, what vanity! But Abraham, who was a real Initiate, didn't rebel, he remained obedient to the will of God, and he prepared to sacrifice his son. As God is not bloodthirsty, as He is not a monster, at the last minute He had Isaac replaced by a ram. Abraham then knew how far his love for the Lord went, of what sacrifice he was capable, and it was enough. A mother who is not ready to act like Abraham, first of all is not an intelligent mother, and secondly, she is too proud. In her ignorance she thinks she knows better than the Lord whether her child should live or die. With her conception of love, even if the child lives, he will bring her much sorrow, because instead of bringing the child closer to the light, she is taking him away from it. In her way of thinking, it is her love that is in first place. She thinks her love is everything, but she will have to pay for this mistake in one way or another, because she will not have done her duty. Her duty is to be in Heaven with her child beside her.

One should never leave Heaven for anyone, not for a child, not for a woman, nor for a husband. It is only by remaining steadfastly faithful to Heaven that you can do them good. If you leave the light to please somebody, you will be attracting nothing but trouble, because in that way you will gain neither Heaven nor earth, which means you will have neither the Lord nor the people for whom you made such a great sacrifice, you will be alone. If it is always a question of sentimentality which predominates, if it is a blind attachment, sooner or later you will suffer. In order to avoid suffering, you should put intelligence, wisdom, and God in first place, and then everything you love will belong to you. All the children that you love properly, purely and divinely, are your children and not the children of their own mother if she loves them the wrong way. You say: "But that's not possible! The blood ties . . ." But those ties are not the most powerful, believe me, for there are ties and ties. Only those men, women and children whom you know how to love belong to you. In appearance the ties of the flesh are the most powerful, but it often happens that the members of a family have no affinity one for the other because they belong to another family, their spiritual family. You can for example, belong physically to a family of peasants and spiritually to a royal family. And on the other hand, you may be physically the child of a royal family, whereas actually you belong to a wretched family of beggars.

Now let us look at someone who loves his family, what will he do? He will have the courage to leave it sometimes to go to another country to earn some money. Someone else, without that love, will lack the courage to leave. In appearance, the first one abandoned his family, but in order to help it; he went away to bring back a fortune and when he returns, everyone is happy. Whereas the one who wouldn't leave his family, remains poor along with them. To explain: A true father or mother will abandon their child or their family and will go to a foreign country, which means the divine world, where they will gather riches, and when they return, they will all be affluent. And the parent who doesn't understand this will stay close to the family, but what will he be able to give them? Not much, a few crumbs, a few trifles of little value. The real father and mother go "abroad". For how long? It depends, for a half-hour perhaps, or an hour, maybe even a day, or three months, and when they return, they distribute their wealth. So you see, I have the strongest arguments that will not be upset by you and all your logic. And if there are mothers who don't agree, let them come and argue with me! I will tell them: "You pretend to love your child, but analyse this love. If you really love him, you will go 'abroad', at least for ten minutes, and if you do that, yes, your child will be taken care of abundantly." And perhaps it is here at the Bonfin,* this foreign country, that you should come and earn a fortune, that is, the knowledge and enlightenment that you will later distribute to your family.

Real love is when the person wants to bring the others close to the Lord. The other kinds of love are nothing but contrivances and scheming, with selfish motives. Sometimes you become friends with someone, you are kind to him and give him presents, but it it is for a reason, to obtain his protection, or benefit in some way from his position in society. Rarely do humans act

---

* One of the centres of the Brotherhood in France.

unselfishly. Even when they give, there is some plan in the back of their minds, there is a reason for the gift. Of course there is always a reason, even the love of the great Masters is for a reason. The Initiates also want to obtain favours, they long for the love and protection of the Lord. Yes, but then it is no longer a question of earthly gain, material acquisition. Initiates seek the glory of God, and that is the only valid reason: to become like the Lord, to shine as He does, to create as He does.

I will not say that my love is absolutely disinterested and unselfish, I can only say that I have made a substitution, the subject and the object are different. It is in our own interest to love the Lord because in so doing we obtain eternal life, light and liberty . . . but it is not really self-interest because these are divine acquisitions . . . eternal life, light and liberty are divine things to seek. So, you see, you have self-interest, but at the same time you fight against selfishness. You try to conquer the inferior ambition in order to have a higher ambition. If you seek only to satisfy your lusts and instincts and your personality, of course that is a lower form of self-interest, but if you have other needs to satisfy, the need for light, for life eternal, for divinity, then it is a higher form of self-interest and there lies the difference. There is a lower form and a higher form of self-interest, but there is always an interest at stake. We are told that it is wrong to be self-concerned. Actually we should change our vocabulary and not refer to unconcern but to a higher form of self-concern.

Now, dear brothers and sisters, if there are still more questions that need clarifying, don't worry, it will come. Here you are in a school, and each day there is a programme, with problems to be solved. You should study hard, so that all the other problems that bother you may also be solved. But don't worry. For the moment, think only about the question of love: how to love your family, how to love your children, only that.

Le Bonfin, August 10, 1963

Chapter XXV

The Meaning of Renunciation

The Maître reads the thought for the day:
"When a bottle is full, is it possible to add more liquid? The bottle must first be emptied. It is the same with humans. If man doesn't empty himself of his vices, his pernicious habits, how can virtues and divine qualities come and install themselves within him? He is already full! That is the meaning of renunciation: to empty oneself, to renounce certain habits, to give up smoking for instance, or lying or slandering, in order to make room for something else. As soon as you get rid of a fault, instantly a quality comes to take its place. This is a law of physics. How can one fill someone with qualities if he is already full of vices? There is no way. He may live near the greatest Master of humanity all his life, but if he doesn't empty himself so that he can be refilled, he will remain the same."

Those who have understood the meaning of renunciation know that it is for themselves that they renounce, so as to create a void into which the divine qualities can be poured. As long as man doesn't understand that, he says to himself: "If I don't smoke anymore, if I can't go to a bar or a night club when I want, I will be too miserable." But no, on the contrary, if he is able to renounce these minor pleasures, they will be replaced by much greater pleasures belonging to a higher order.

It's very simple. You cannot fill a bottle if it is already full. Of course if it is filled with the elixir of immortal life, you mustn't empty it, but if it contains nothing but grime and mildew, why preserve it? Unfortunately, humans know how to fill themselves with filth but they don't know how to empty themselves of it. Starting with their childhood, they are surrounded by people who are not really the models to follow, who transmit their habits and ways of thinking and acting that are entirely wrong. And now, in order to empty themselves of all that, in order to renew and rejuvenate themselves, in order to change the impression and break the mould, they must look for other models, they must find people who are like the sun, who are themselves little suns. In the world everybody looks for a career, a family, a house full of comfort, and that's enough for them, they are satisfied with a mediocre life. From time to time, they will read a few books, listen to some records, take a walk, go to a party now and then and that's all. In this way they don't advance, they are adding nothing new to their lives, nothing more important and enlightening, and they are not aware of the dangers of this life in slow motion. All the psychic and physical illnesses are waiting for the right moment to slip in and bite them and eat into them. Cosmic Intelligence didn't go to the trouble of forming such a wonderful creature as man for the purpose of letting him sleep his life away, chloroformed. It planned for him to advance without ceasing on the path of evolution, to release an intense current of life that casts off all the impurities. Otherwise the dirt accumulates and he sinks down into the mire.

People often ask me about the question of purity in love, when love is pure and when it is impure. The answer is easy. Look at Nature: all that is soiled, impure, tarnished, has a tendency to go downwards, and all that is pure rises to the heights. It is the same for the human being, that which is gross within him gathers in the lower places and everything that is light, pure and shining climbs up into his head. This is why the eyes, ears, mouth, nose and brain are above, and other things are lower down. To these two divisions of man, the lower and the upper, correspond his two natures, the inferior and the superior, the personality and the individuality. Love as it is manifested by the personality cannot be pure, as the personality is connected to the subterranean world, and this love is full of selfish elements, dense and dark. The love of the personality thinks only of taking, of conquering, and so it is not pure. For the blind, all is pure, but not for the Initiates who see the emanations, the radiations, the colours of each thought and each feeling. Love that is coarse, primitive and sensual cannot be pure. Whereas the love of the individuality is pure because it contains other elements, generosity, intelligence, gentleness, unselfishness.

Through their love, humans give each other all kinds of filth which prevents them from seeing clearly and from experiencing heavenly sensations. They create barriers made up of layers of selfish and sensual love. People are free to follow their inclinations, but that doesn't mean they are right. The Initiates who left us rules and instructions were not trying to bar the road to love and make humans ill, but they were trying to prevent them from going down too low into the infernal regions where they would lose everything. When man allows himself to be dominated by the personality, the circle of his activities and his consciousness is reduced, and not only does he become stupid and blind but he no longer receives the blessings and wonders of the divine world.

Selfish love is always impure. And so, love as it is practiced by most humans at the moment is not pure, and the exchanges men and women spend their time making are full of illness and vice. Everybody knows how to live that kind of love which is so ordinary, but it takes thousands of years to explain the other kind, people don't understand it, they have no clear idea and the more explanations they hear, the more obscure it becomes, because there is something missing inside, they are not prepared.

In Initiatic Science it is said that privation in reality is not a privation but a replacement, a transposition into another world. The same activity continues, but with materials of such purity and light that there is no danger. For example, one denies oneself the experience of love on the physical plane in order to experience love on a higher plane; where it is better. Furthermore, if one renounces something without going to draw from another source, without breathing or eating in a higher place, it is dangerous, because one becomes inhibited. When one says that one should deprive oneself, that one should make sacrifices, it is only a manner of speech. In reality one shouldn't deprive oneself, one should simply move away to a higher region to continue doing whatever one did below ... instead of drinking water in a swamp full of germs, drink crystalline water from a pure spring. But not to drink at all is to accept death. No, one must not stop drinking, but one must give up drinking the water of the gutter in exchange for the waters of Heaven.

Actually an Initiate is deprived of nothing, he eats, drinks, breathes, and loves, but in realms and states of consciousness unknown to the ordinary man. When they hear the word renunciation, people are appalled and think: "But if I renounce certain things I'll die." And this is true, they will die. If they can't understand that they must renounce something in order to have something far better, they will die. We must drink, sleep, breathe, love and create children, but we must do all those things in a better way, and to learn to do them better, there exists a whole science which is unknown. You see how clear it is, you need not suppress or repress, you must transpose, you must sublimate.

All the inferior tendencies, then, need to be replaced by other tendencies, other habits and needs of a higher quality. The way most people generally try to get rid of their habit of smoking, drinking, or their need for women, is by suppressing the desire without putting something else in its place, and this is extremely dangerous for they are thrown off balance, and are plunged into a void. There must be a compensation, you must substitute a higher desire to take the place of the lower desire. That is why those who have kept themselves from loving have not really understood, instead they should replace the object of their love by another object, a more luminous object, or else it means death. Nature has organized things well, we eat, we drink, we breathe and none of those things need to be suppressed, we need only refine our needs or transpose them onto a higher plane.

Think well each time you decide to give up a need that is very strong within you, for it is a serious decision to make. The need should be replaced, and to satisfy it, you should go on eating, drinking, loving and living, but on a level and to a degree that no longer exposes you to the same dangers. You will succumb unless you put something else in place of your habitual needs.

Take someone who needs women for instance, how can he conquer his desire? Strangely enough, with women. Instead of limiting himself to one, he must become interested in all women simultaneously, and that will save him. Instead of wallowing in the clutches of one woman who will ruin him, he should be thinking: "I must love all the women in the world!" And since he can't behave badly with that many women at once, he will be saved, because he loves womanhood in all women, and this love will bring him happiness and peace. And women can use the same method. Instead of loving one man, they can learn to love all men, and all men will fill them with joy, happiness and inspiration. As long as they can't realize this widening of their consciousness, they will be unhappy, and eventually become bitter and petty. Remember this method. If you don't replace the desire you have, or the attraction, the weakness, the passion or the vice, with another desire, another attraction of a higher quality, you will be divided, always in conflict with yourself, don't forget that. Even if you have lost the person you love, if he has abandoned you or died, you must replace him ... not by someone else whom you run the risk of losing also, but by a great love for something celestial and divine. Then calm and peace will be yours because the inner void has been filled. People like to replace a husband, wife or lover with some other husband, wife, or lover, but that is never the answer.

No matter how much I explain all this to you, it will never

be really clear until you have made it clear within yourselves through meditation, and until you have made inner
adjustments. Everything that is clear to me is perhaps not yet
clear to you, because you have another structure, another vision
of things. It is up to you to do the necessary work to clarify what I
tell you. When you have done this, you will have all that Nature
meant you to have, you will be able to make use of that which
you have, with as much precision as if you were in a laboratory or
a power station, and you will be able to manipulate the forces
and currents without ever being overcome, without any harm to
yourselves. And at that moment, Nature gives you the right to do
as you will with men and women, with the entire world. But at
the same time something unusual happens to you, and you
yourself will have no desire to take advantage of this right: your
sense of beauty, your desire for perfection, for illumination, for
purity, will be so highly developed that you will no longer wish to
descend into certain regions which are too close to Hell, and you
will prefer to remain in the higher regions where you feel at
home.

I will tell you a story. One day, walking about his realm, a king
saw a cow in a field, and this cow seemed to him so marvellous
that he wished to purchase it. He sent one of his servants to deal
with the cow's owner, but this owner was a mage, an old wise
man, and he refused to sell his cow, for she gave him the milk
that was his only sustenance, and he didn't wish to be separated
from her. The servant returned with his reply, and the king then
decided to take the cow by force. He sent several members of his
retinue to seize her, but the sage held out his hand and paralyzed
them momentarily, and then sent them away. "Tell your
master", he said, "that there is nothing doing, he is rich and
powerful and he should leave me my cow which is all I have."
The king, furious, sent a whole army to get the cow, but again the
mage froze them where they stood and sent them back as he had
done before. So the king began to think: "This sage must have a
very great knowledge since he has so much power, I will go and

rob him of his secret." He disguised himself and presented himself to the mage: "Venerable old man", he said, "your reputation for wisdom is great throughout the land and I have come to learn from you. Accept me as your disciple." Of course the mage recognized the king and read his thoughts, but he didn't show it, and agreed to teach the king. For years the king remained, to learn how to meditate, how to breathe, he prayed and fasted . . . and one day, thinking about the cow, he realized that he no longer wanted it! He had become wise himself, and had no more desire to own the cow.

If you can say to yourself: "I want all the women in the world", and make every effort to become good and attractive and appealing, exercising yourself in meditation and prayer, then in the end, your desire will vanish before the discoveries you will make. You will live in a magnificent world which you will not want to leave. That is what we must do. There are some people in the world who have completely overcome sensuality, but this is very rare, it is only the great Initiates. They could do anything, they are allowed anything they wish, but they don't wish to come down from the heights they have reached.

Now, dear brothers and sisters, you must reflect on what you have just heard, and understand that a divine philosophy exists which is able to give you everything. Only you must wish it, you must accept it, and become involved in it. Humans think that they know everything and they don't want to learn a thing, but I am going to show you bit by bit the true value of what you know and where it will lead you, and then you will be horrified to see that you have been swaggering around, proud as a peacock, but of what? Of your ignorance. As we say in Bulgaria: "Na gol toumbac srebarni pichtofi", which means: "Naked except for two silver pistols". Nothing but a pair of pistols with which to face the entire world!

Le Bonfin, August 18, 1975

Chapter XXVI

The Bonds of Love

The Maître reads the thought for the day:

"Human beings have cut the bond between each other and this severance, this break has brought them hatred, hostility, enmity, vengeance and anarchy. Look at the Arab countries and Israël, Vietnam and the U.S. You will say: "But the bonds aren't cut if they are throwing bombs at each other!" It's true that the bonds are not cut on the physical plane, they are closer than ever in order to kill each other, but I am speaking of the spiritual plane, that is where the bonds are severed and this act of severance is called war.

Of course in war there are bonds. Take two people who detest each other, they have never been closer, but it's in order to stab each other! And others who are separated by thousands of kilometres have a closer bond than ever. When I speak of bonds, I see them as something used by mechanics and electricians. The mechanism doesn't work because a few centimetres of wire are lacking. I come along, I add a little bit of wire, and it works, the current is on again, the mechanism functions: it all depends on one little thing: the connecting bond."

This is not a new subject for you, dear brothers and sisters, you have already heard me speak about bonds. Everything that exists in the universe is connected, our physical body is nothing but a system of connecting bonds with different names according to their functions: hair, filaments, veins, canals, vessels, arteries, and these intricate threads form tissues . . . you know all that. If you were clairvoyant you would see that men and women are entangled in bonds, threads that go off in all directions. And they think they can be separate from each other, that they can be free and independent! Merely by thinking about someone you create a bond, thoughts are nothing but that, bonds, connecting threads. If you want to harm someone, your thought is a rope, a lassoo that you throw around him to snare him and destroy him. But if you are full of love for him, your thought is a channel, a duct through which you nourish him, it is a bond that you create between him and all that is best for him, to help him and enlighten him. Whether it be love or hate, thoughts and feelings create bonds.

People talk about the bonds of love, but there are also the bonds of hate. When you think about someone constantly, wondering how you can do him the most harm, your hatred is creating bonds which bind you fast to him for who knows how long a time, perhaps for several incarnations. In your desire to rid yourself of him, you are creating the most formidable bond. Hatred is a bond, love is a bond, you meet over and over again the ones you love and hate. To have no more bonds at all with anyone, you must feel neither hatred nor love, but indifference. Thus, to rid yourself of an enemy, at least try to be indifferent to him, otherwise your hatred will bring all kinds of trouble down on your own head. And love also, if it is not a pure, spiritual, unselfish love, will bring you nothing but problems.

Let's talk a little more about love since this subject is the most interesting one, the most important and the most current, and there is no one who doesn't think about it, no one, whether man or woman, young or old. When we think of hating, it is clear, there is nothing to be said except for the disastrous results it can entail, which is something we don't realize. But when it is a question of love, nobody understands. It is such a rich and complex field with so many different aspects that have never been properly explained . . . Look at how long I have been speaking to you about love! I will try again today to bring you this subject in the hope that I can finally make it clear.

The whole world thinks it normal to love each other, to marry and have children. Nothing seems more natural. No one is surprised when you fall in love because everyone comes down with the same illness. That is why people think it so strange and abnormal to want to make changes and bring humans up to the higher levels; they are surprised and hostile to change. And this is where I will now try to throw a little light. As I have explained in other talks, it was cosmic Intelligence who gave humans the instinct to love, the same as with animals. But this state was not meant to last forever, cosmic Intelligence had other plans in mind for them, a more evolved state, more spiritual. These two tendencies are represented in man by his inferior nature, or the personality, which thinks only of taking, of satisfying his needs; and his superior nature, the individuality, which thinks about the needs and the happiness of others. You can see some manifestations of this kind in animals and wild beasts, maternal or paternal instincts which make parents think about their young and find food for them, protect them and even sacrifice themselves for them. These manifestations are proof that cosmic Intelligence has placed in each living creature this quality that is however not yet well developed, because, by defending his progeny, the animal is actually defending his own possessions. With humans the same thing is somewhat true, but nevertheless their higher nature is more highly developed, and the saints, the Martyrs, the great Masters for instance, have given un-questionable proof of sacrifice and self-abnegation.

If you read Volume XI which deals with the question of the personality and the individuality, you will have a very clear idea of the way in which these two natures manifest themselves all day long through your thoughts, feelings, actions and attitude, and you will see how often you are inspired by the personality: always seeing the bad side of people, always suspicious, always doubtful.

And even when you are with an Initiate, a Master who can show you your errors and the gaps in your knowledge, you won't accept his way of looking at things. Instead of saying: "O Master, you are probably right, I didn't know things were as you describe them, but I trust you, since you have gone so much further than I . . .", some people refuse to accept what the Master says to help them, and hold on to their limited point of view. Under those conditions, how can they ever improve?

But it is especially in the realm of love that the two natures are apparent – the personality and the individuality. A boy may think he loves a girl when actually he loves himself, and thinks only of satisfying himself at the expense of her beauty and purity, her youth and freshness, and then, once he's had his fill, he throws her away like a used lemon peel to go looking for someone fresher. Someone else might think only of the girl, of how to help her and protect and teach her, and plan for her future. This love is rare but it does exist, and that is the love of the individuality. Now here is the most important point, listen carefully.

From now on, when you love someone, observe yourself to see what your needs are, and you will discover that what you thought was normal and natural, beyond reproach, since the whole world feels that way, was actually inspired by the personality. At that instant make the decision to stop living so much in sensations, in constant turmoil, volcanic eruptions, and to use part of your energy for your evolution, to understand and improve yourself. Put the individuality to work and your love will carry you all the way to Heaven and all its glory. With the other kind of love, you become heavy, coarse and brutish, without light, without inspiration, and you are harmful to others. There, it's plain and clear, you may wish to say that you are not in agreement, but that doesn't keep it from being the truth.

That the personality's way of loving is normal and natural, of course I agree, I never said that it was not, but what is natural for the personality is unnatural for the individuality, who is standing by, waiting to manifest itself, to come into its own. As long as you

remain with your primitive instincts, you hamper the individuality, you keep it from manifesting. I don't say that instinctive
love has no reason to exist, and for those who enjoy it, let them
have it, but I have always been for progress. I am for going
further and higher, not to stop loving but to take love a step
higher. I often compare the human being to a skyscraper with a
hundred, a hundred and fifty floors: the tenants on the ground
floor have water to drink but the others die of thirst because
nothing reaches them. One needs pressure to bring the water all
the way to the top floors, and that's the trouble, as soon as
there is a little pressure, one rushes to relieve it with some man
or woman, and there is nothing left for the top floor. You see
how ignorant one can be! This pressure is needed to bring the
water to the brain, but you say you can't help it, you can't stand
it, you must get rid of it . . . You should rejoice that such a thing
exists, and you should conserve it because it allows you to
nourish those inanimate cells up there in the brain. Without that
water, you become an idiot, a brute. The cells of the brain need
water.

If some of you are not yet convinced, too bad for you. The
others want to progress, they seek more and more information
and enlightenment. I am speaking for them, and I say there is a
way to do it. What way? I was speaking before about bonds, the
threads and channels. Are you familiar with the extraordinary
system cosmic Intelligence installed thousands of years ago in the
human being? If this system doesn't work it is because humans
make no attempt to direct their energies, to make use of this
subtle, etheric mechanism. Furthermore, who is there today who
even knows that man has this special system, this network of
channels which makes it possible for the sexual forces to circulate
as far as the brain? Sexual force is extraordinarily powerful, and
when it nourishes the physical body, at the same time it feeds the
personality with feelings of hatred and war. Sexual force is able
to accomplish wonders, it can be used for formidable purposes,
but until now it has only been used as the means of furthering

human separation and hostility. Inferior love is close to aggressivity. One who is steeped in sensuality is also steeped in force and aggressivity. The higher form of love concentrates on spiritual conquests. It will still be Venus inspiring Mars, but they each have two aspects, the higher and the lower. Superior love, or Venus in her higher aspect, awakens the higher aspect of Mars who then marches forth to explore the divine world and bring his knowledge back to earth.

So, my dear brothers and sisters, what are you going to do with what I have just told you? Not much, I know. You have taken notes which you will leave somewhere and you will go on feeding the inferior nature until there is nothing left. And I know you will say: "Oh, Maître, we agree, we understand, we feel that what you say is true, but you don't know how hard it is for us to do." I know very well how hard it is, but the fact that you know it is true will make it possible for you to do it. If you don't know about it you will never do it. It is better therefore to talk to you about it, and even if you are incapable of realizing such splendour, you will be able to keep trying until one day you will have overcome the obstacles that prevented you from succeeding.

One of these obstacles is fear, fear based on ignorance. You think you will be deprived of all joy and satisfaction. There will be privation to a certain extent of course, but you will be exchanging weakness for strength, absurdity for intelligence, you will be depriving yourself of something that brings you worries and tragedy in order to move towards something that will bring you peace and happiness. Do you think that I am deprived of anything whatsoever? I am not so stupid as to be deprived of anything ... and deprived I am not, I have replaced one thing by another. You will say: "But you don't smoke." Oh! I smoke other things, celestial things, wonderful things. And the wine I drink, if you only knew! We need to deprive ourselves of a tiny pleasure in order to have the right to taste a much greater one.

I will stop there, but think about this subject. And think also about the question of bonds. In the universe, everything is connected: the sun, the stars, the planets, the trees, stones and crystals, atoms and electrons which are formed according to lines of force, geometric figures, and people's faces, everything is linked together. And take the physical body, it is nothing other than the tissues you have woven yourself, beautiful or ugly, bright or sombre, symmetric or assymmetric, everything is woven, that is why it is so important to be terribly careful when you are forming bonds with people and things, because you are weaving your own clothing for a future incarnation. It is a whole science. And when you don't know how to weave, you are bound to make stupid mistakes, acts of folly. If you make ties with a criminal, you will have to suffer with him, pay the price he pays, because you are associates, partners, you participate and collaborate with him in whatever he does. But people never think about this, they become friends with anyone, even the Devil. Reflect a bit, and try only to make close ties with people who are evolved, radiant people, the Initiates, the Angels and Archangels, the Divinities, otherwise you will never know any peace, all your life, everything will be dark and frightening.

This question of bonds between people goes further than you imagine. Each thought and each feeling, each promise is a bond. And look: though they may not tie you with rope, you are nevertheless tied down by contracts and signatures and agreements; if you have signed, you are bound and no court can get you out of it. These bonds exist even more terrifyingly on the astral and mental planes where people think only of binding each other hand and foot so as to profit from each other. Those are the most difficult bonds to cut even though they can't be seen. Are you convinced? Meditate on this, be conscious of its importance, and be very careful: your very life is at stake.

Le Bonfin, August 17, 1975

Chapter XXVII

Youth and the Problem of Love –
The New Currents

The world must be able to understand, interpret and apply the
new light, the new understanding that is about to appear. The
proof that it is coming is that everything is in motion. It has
never been this way before. Take youth, this youth that refuses to
walk in the footsteps of the adults. They alone prove that God is
creating a new Heaven and a new earth, because it is through
humans that revolutions occur. The young look for happiness
through sexual freedom. They are not to be blamed, on the
contrary, it is a sign that new ideas are being formed. At the
moment, obviously, things are not as they should be. One
shouldn't imagine that all innovations are wonderful and that
one should accept them. No, a wise and enlightened authority
must weigh, revise and sanction them.

At the moment, there are nothing but revolts, turmoil, forces
bubbling up, but nothing is organized; that is the work that
needs to be done. It is like the time of the formation of the earth,
when the volcanic eruptions tore apart the earth's crust that was
barely solidified. Life was impossible on earth then for either
vegetables or animals, let alone for humans. All those forces had
to calm down and the intelligences had to come and organize
things for the earth to be habitable for plants, animals, and men.
And there are a great many men who have an inner life like the
earth in its early primitive state, with anger, revolt and
uncontrolled sexual energies that erupt exactly like volcanic
eruptions, and these are indicative of man's age: they show that
he still lives in the era when the earth was too unsafe for

intelligent beings to work there. As long as man shelters within
him brute forces, the primitive forces, and gives them free rein,
he is considered an uncertain, unreliable being by angels,
Archangels and Initiates, who leave him alone, and give him time
to calm down before they bring him their light and their wisdom.
When the same being becomes reasonable, when he controls
himself, then he is like the earth in its present state, and then they
take care of him, his soil is prepared, seeds are planted, great care
is taken and the result is a civilization, a culture, a whole
humanity that installs itself in him, in the shape of angels and
magnificent entities.

The present state of society shows that the forces which
manifest themselves now are neither oriented nor organized, but
this will come. People will come who will organize the currents
that are now colliding and clashing with each other. The new
Heaven is already here, and the new light is beginning to make its
way, so when you hear of strange things happening in the world,
do not worry.

Take youth for instance, it has never before been the way it is
now. In the past, youth was more docile and obedient. I don't say
that it was marvellous, no, it was different. Now, youth delights
in not conforming. In every field it asserts itself and shows its
independence, which will at least serve to make adults think.

The young think that by insisting on sexual freedom their lives
will be full of success, joy and happiness. But it's not true! It is
because they don't know the structure of the human being that
they think this way, and this ignorance will end up destroying
their equilibrium, their health and their minds. I don't say that
they should repress all desire, no, that would break them, for
sexual force is a most ancient inherent force which is impossible
to overcome. Therefore I am not advising repression, to be
inhibited is not the answer, nor is the answer complete liberty,
because that will bring other kinds of trouble. With true
Initiation, you learn that this force is not to be fought against but
to be directed. When parents pick on their children for their

faults, they fail, because you mustn't oppose these things directly, instead they must be used and canalized and sent in another direction. But, because parents are ignorant, children take no notice of what they say, they don't even listen.

Parents haven't bothered to instruct their sons and daughters on the subject of sex, especially years ago when it was the tradition for children to be utterly ignorant. It's only in the last few years that sexual education has been sanctioned, and this does not always mean progress, because everyone rushes to talk about something they don't yet know anything about.

The other evening I was looking at a programme on television where there was a discussion between parents, teachers and doctors as to the best way to explain to children how babies are born. They showed a film in which a mother told her nine year old son exactly what happens. I was stupefied to see how she went about telling him, with what a lack of psychology. She gave him all kinds of technical terminology, spoke about periods of fertility, the process of ovulation and so forth and the poor child, wide-eyed, understood not one word . . . I was sorry for him . . . And she went on to explain bluntly the role of the father, impregnation, pregnancy, and the details of how the baby came into the world. The boy in all his innocence listened but obviously with no understanding.

That is not the way to handle this problem, I would have done it differently. First I would have shown the child the world of plants and flowers, showing him that a flower is fertilized by pollen, and explaining how fruit is formed. And then I would have told him about insects and animals, showing him what happens in Nature, in the fields. The child would then have understood all the rest by himself, and it would have been more poetic than describing how the man's organ becomes hard in order to penetrate the woman. The mother had the best intentions but nevertheless failed. There are so many other fields in which humans are awkward, unable to obtain good results!

It is obvious that the pill has brought progress in the world, specially in the United States and the Nordic countries, and even in India and the Arab countries. At first it was there because of the population explosion, but afterwards it was for other reasons having nothing to do with population, but more with the need for enjoyment without any hindrance on anyone's part. Is it really necessary for a girl of fifteen to use the pill? They do use them however, and in some schools it is the teachers who distribute them to the pupils, yes, the teachers.

I am not an advocate of asceticism, but neither am I for licentiousness. By allowing the young to rush into this region of which they know nothing, we are opening the door for them to all kinds of physical and psychic derangement. They make their experiments without realizing that in the long run, this will make them unbalanced and ill. Actually, neither those who permit the pill nor those who oppose it have understood what it means. Those who came out in favour did so because they knew that humans are weak and they capitulated to this weakness, and the others, the hypocrites, are opposed to the pill because they are for the old traditions even though they don't respect them any more.

Every feeling, all excitement, each volcanic eruption results in the burning of energy; humans act as though their energies were inexhaustible. But no, everything is planned, each creature that is born on earth is given a reserve of energy, and if that creature is not reasonable, if he wastes those reserves, too bad, he will not be given any more. And the proof is that sometimes a person needs just a drop of life in order to finish his work and yet it is not given to him. Humans draw on their energies as if from an unlimited ocean, they think they can do anything they want. No, it is all calculated. With the pretext that the pill is now here, people no longer use brakes or measures, they don't know that they are burning up their reserves, their brain matter, and in a little while they will deteriorate and lose all intellectual power. Now that the pill is there they think it is no longer necessary to think or to use control, to master themselves. No, no, close your eyes and let yourself go!

If humans are always ready to waste the energy of love, it is because the whole world is used to thinking only about the needs of the personality. We don't spend our time making collective, glorious, divine plans, we seek only our own good, our pleasure, and it seems normal to us to look for it where we can find satisfaction. That's all very well, but we behave like animals. If we have any desire to become more than that, we cannot be content with just satisfying the personality, we must also satisfy the individuality, the divine side, we must have some other purpose beside our own pleasure. Because pleasure narrows man's circle of action to such an extent that he is himself reduced, ignominious to the point of being overlooked completely. There is another kind of work that you must do if you wish others to take notice.

When I say these things to the young that are here, when I speak of their future and all the complications that await them if they continue in the same direction, there are many who decide to change and you can have no idea what joy that gives me. What a joy to know that the young are seeking the good, but without knowing where to look. It's not so much their fault, nobody has told them, but still they are looking for something great and fine and good. This is why I like working with young people so much.

And now to finish, I will say this to them: if you are in love, good, but try not to devour the object of your devotion, because it could be that in the middle of these great outbursts of emotion, you might grow tired, begin to see the bad side, be disappointed, and lose your joy and your inspiration. Why must you go down so far into the sewer, all the way to Hell, to know about everything? Content yourselves with beauty, and the beauty will never end. But humans in their weakness want to know everything right away and then destroy it. That's why after a little time they are no longer inspired, they don't even want to see each other: because they saw each other too much, they tasted and ate too much and now they are sated. And it's all over, the great love is finished. This love brought them all the blessings, it brought them Heaven, yet they sacrificed all that for the sake of a few minutes of enjoyment. Why not try to retain themselves as long as possible to benefit from something so inspiring, this elixir of immortal life that they are drinking? But no, they're in a hurry to get to the end, but the end will not be good. Even if they marry and have children and go on living together, it will be from habit, out of respect for conventions, to put up a good front before parents and friends, but inside, they have left each other long ago. It is the subtle feelings that maintain love, that beautify and prolong life, that give us strength.

Sèvres, January 1, 1967

Marriage

Nature has so created humans that they all require affection and tenderness, they have a need for exchanges. It is a universal need, no one can escape or object.

Take a young girl for instance, she needs affection, and she quickly chooses a boy to love, without thinking about the kind of character she would most appreciate in a partner. In order to satisfy her need, she has to accept all the rest that goes with the boy, his thoughts and feelings, which are perhaps vulgar, and his character, with which she is not always in accord. Of course he gives her something, but because of what he gives her, she must take all the rest. This is the way it is with all boys and girls. For a few sensations, a few crumbs of joy, they are stuck with all sorts of inconveniences and difficulties, and they complain for the rest of their lives that they are unhappy and don't know what to do. To get out of such a situation, many laws will have to be broken.

So you see, dear brothers and sisters, it is sad but true: for a few satisfactions, everybody gets buried under endless complications. They feel a need, and because of the need for a few crumbs, they are obliged to accept all kinds of impurity, including the warped condition of the one who gives the crumbs. You might at least look for someone who is pure, radiant, noble, and if such a person can't be found, at least be patient, don't marry anyone, for if you do, you will pay dearly. Unfortunately there are not many who want to preserve their purity in order to accomplish something tremendous, all is forgotten for the sake of a few sexual sensations.

You, the young, should at least be aware of what criterion has been given by the Initiates before throwing yourselves lightly into the first amorous adventure that presents itself. It is better to wait, to be patient, until you can find a being with whom you have an affinity, who can complete you from every point of view, even magically, and under those conditions, go ahead, have your experiences, get married, have children! If you can't find the person who is your complement, it isn't worth having adventure after adventure with no matter whom, for the price you will have to pay is too high. Wait, search, and when you have found this person, when your entire being vibrates in unison with God and there is a love that only the poets have been able to describe, then, yes. But to go and have ten, twenty, a hundred experiences, to wear oneself out, to soil oneself, to backslide, really is a shame and you should refuse. If it is love you want, let it be real love or nothing at all!

This is my advice to the young: Don't be in a hurry, don't rush to ruin your lives with the first one to appear. First, study the situation, try to see this question of love clearly, and then go ahead, go and seek your beloved. But first of all, take care to find out whether this person is really prepared to work with you and walk with you in the same direction, otherwise you will spend your lives mutually destroying each other. Examine the situation thoroughly to see whether you are really in accord on the three planes, physically, emotionally, intellectually, or if you are attracted only by pleasure. If you both have entirely different opinions on important subjects, don't think: "Oh, it doesn't matter, we'll get along, in the long run we will agree." It will be the contrary. In a short time, when you are tired of certain pleasures, when your feelings have become blunted, you will see that your ideas and tastes are all too different, and this difference brings on the arguments, the heartbreaks, the separations. Being in agreement on the plane of ideas and tastes is very important. Physical attraction, even when there is also a little love, is not enough, we become too quickly sated and blasé. And if intelligence is missing, if there is no way of having an interesting conversation, full of fresh ideas, then lovers will become bored with each other.

There are people who don't love each other physically but who adore each other because they always have a million things to say to each other, things to explain and stories to tell, it's wonderful! The ideal is to agree on all three planes, to have a mutual physical attraction, a similarity of tastes and feelings, because if one prefers noise and the other prefers silence, if one likes to read and the other to dance, if one likes to go out and the other likes to stay home, there will be fighting! Finally, and most important of all, there must be a tremendous agreement in the world of ideas, a common goal, an ideal. If this harmony exists on the three planes, there is nothing more marvellous than the union of these two people, because they are to each other an inexhaustible source of joy, happiness, and understanding.

Unfortunately young men and women do not have such criteria. They take these things too lightly, they are too much in a hurry, and they leave too much to chance in the choice of a partner. Suppose you have a bag full of adders, lizards, doves, crocodiles and mice . . . You say: "I'm going to plunge my hand in, and surely I'll draw out a dove." Because you weren't looking, your hand is bitten by an adder. It is naïve to think that you can trust to blind luck to give you a dove or a love bird. People imagine that Providence is always there to take care of the blind, to help them and save them. Not so, as soon as Providence sees someone is blind, she takes to her heels and leaves them to destiny, and destiny's job is to punish them. But if Providence sees two people trying to use their eyes, she says: "Ah, that is what I like to see, I am going to help them." The strangest thing is that some blind people, after being bitten by an adder, go looking for the same adder in order to be bitten a second time. And I have seen women so stubborn as to say: "I am going to start again with the same man, maybe he'll improve." Who has ever seen a snake or a crocodile who could improve himself?

Physical attraction is important, of course, but it is not the most important. How many times have there been people who adored each other one minute, and detested each other a little while later? And yet they haven't changed physically. A boy for instance, loses his head over a pretty girl, ravishing from every angle, and he marries her. Some time later, he discovers that she is frivolous, unfaithful, capricious, and stupid, and he loves her less and less, and is so disgusted with what he sees her to be inside, that even her beauty no longer appeals to him. The contrary is also true. A boy meets a girl who is not terribly pretty, but after a time, he is so enchanted by her wisdom, her kindness, her patience and her unselfish spirit that little by little she wins him completely. All other girls fade before this girl who didn't at first seem attractive, because inside, she is marvellous, faithful, well-balanced, honest, always there to patch up his wounds, comfort him, and give him good advice. The physical side no longer counts for him, he adores her, and when he introduces her to his friends who pity him or criticize him for his choice, he thinks: "Ah, poor things, they don't know what a treasure I have in my wife!" A lot of men enjoy wearing their wives like a decoration and everyone congratulates them because they don't realize the wife is a shrew who harasses them night and day. She makes a lovely decoration that they are proud to parade so that they can feel envied by the world. They suffer the rest of the time but it doesn't matter, they go to the opera and to parties to show off their wives. Perhaps they only wanted a jewel, but this is a very costly jewel.

I advise boys and girls who want to get married not to make a hurried decision, but to come and study the laws of love. When they have learned how to love each other and how to prepare themselves to have children and educate them, then they can make the decision. But they rush headlong, and afterwards, poor things, when the children are already there, when difficulties and illnesses arrive, they are scared to death, rush to the doctors, read all the books to learn what they need to know, whereas before they had fun and thought: "Oh, there's plenty of time, we'll figure it out later!" No, it's before that you should learn that things must be figured out.

Sometimes a brother of the Fraternity gets married to a pretty girl who is worldy. But then this girl doesn't want to follow the Teaching, she won't hear spirituality mentioned, she wants neither to improve herself nor learn anything. So, poor thing, he finds himself in a complicated situation and sometimes he leaves this School, to please a silly girl. That proves that he was stupid too, and that he will have to suffer. The same thing happens when a sister marries a boy who doesn't want anything to do with her ideas; she is obliged to sacrifice everything that is most marvellous in her heart and soul to please an idiot, and then she's unhappy. This is not the way to solve the problem. Nothing should be done quickly. You say: "But soon we'll be old!" It is better to marry when one is old and choose someone who will be right. Why hurry? So as to grow old sooner through suffering? I see women sometimes three or four years after their marriage, who have become so aged because of worry and hardship that I no longer recognize them. Even if you don't find Prince Charming until your old age, all at once you're rejuvenated . . . even if you are ninety years old, it doesn't matter, you become like a young girl of twenty.

Actually, whether you wait or not, whether you are able to see properly or not, as long as you yourself are not up to scratch, it will be bad, no matter what you do. You should at least be ready, prepared for marriage. Who will accept you if you aren't? You say: "Yes, but I wish to marry a princess, or the Queen of Heaven . . ." Will she want you? Does anyone want a weakling, an incapable idiot, unless they are that way themselves? Let's take a young girl who is ravishing but who can't say anything, she hasn't read much, she doesn't know anything, and she is not able to understand the man she loves, nor amuse him in any way, nor encourage or comfort him, she counts only on his body. Well, whoever he is, he will very quickly tire of her and forget about her. because she had nothing within herself to give his soul or his spirit. Even the best man in the world will make her unhappy, because she has nothing to offer. He might have a taste for the artistic, or the spiritual, and she, having no such taste, will suffer because she will feel inferior. If you haven't perfected yourself in any way, it is better not to become involved with a prince or a princess!

The first thing to do is to prepare yourself, so that come what may, you will be capable of handling the situation, because I am telling you, even with the best partner in the world, nothing will work out, they will leave you for other creatures who are more intelligent, better prepared, and there will be nothing left to do but weep. Prepare yourselves, and make yourself into a store of treasures, precious stones, in other words qualities and abilities so that no one will be your equal. Then, yes, the person you love will stay with you. Why should he go looking for someone else? But never is this question seen in this way. A girl wants a boy, good, but how is she going to keep him? If she is incapable she won't keep him very long. One needs to be prepared; for years and years, one needs to be preparing. You say: "But I will grow old and ugly . . ." It doesn't matter. You will be old and ugly on the exterior perhaps, but so young and beautiful inside that you will keep the prince forever. The work must be done, you must prepare without thinking about time, or age.

The question of love interests everybody, and always will. More and more from now on, mankind will be thinking only about loving, living with love, always looking for love, emanating love. Love will be the centre of everything, all will converge towards love. Science, art, religion, all will have one goal: to spread love, to instil love, to give love. True happiness lies in the desire to give one's love everywhere. But, given the way humans are at the moment, it is very dangerous to give your love unless you are very wise. How many poor girls inspired by generosity have thought of nothing but the happiness of the man they were with, only to be eaten and thrown away as though they were lemon peels! Before showing your love, you should learn to love without letting yourself be devoured, you should be able to say: "The cake is untouched and the guests are satisfied." Which means that you feed the entire world with your love without demagnetizing yourself, and without becoming sad or weary. . . . On the contrary, you become more radiant, more intelligent and stronger. You "nourish the guests" and you remain intact. Without wisdom, it's over, you are well bitten into, and then discarded. This bit of advice is most important for the young.

I said to a young girl one day: "Love the boy you choose to love, but don't tell him. – Why not? – Because it is your love that makes you happy, that moves you forward, that gives meaning to your life, and as this boy is far from perfect, if he knows that you love him, without wanting to, he'll spoil it all . . . you can tell him, but when you are prepared and strong, and he too. Then you no longer run any risk. If not, continue to love him but hide your love. If he were evolved, there would be no danger, but on the level where he is, he will take advantage, he'll say: "Here is an open door, let's go in!" and not a trace of your youth, your freshness would remain. Disappointed, you would say: "He doesn't understand me, I detest him . . ." Love will be finished, and you too will be finished. It's your love that gives you wings and you mustn't sacrifice your love for a boy who doesn't understand you. As long as it is love that gives you wings, continue to love him, but hide it, hide it well. Whether the boy deserves it or not is not what is important. The important thing is that this love should give you the forward impulse, the desire to live, to surmount all obstacles. Don't lose it! Remember always that it is your love that counts, and not the person you love, for it is your love that nourishes you."

Sèvres, April 13, 1968

Why Self-Control

The Maître reads the thought for the day:

"We think of everything that is disturbing to us as the enemy. Well, we should take a look at this enemy. For primitive man, fire was the enemy, as were also lightning, water, the wind, earth, animals ... everything was an enemy, and man fought against them and died. In time, he learned to tame these forces and then he discovered how useful they were.

Man understood something about the elements that can also be applied to other manifestations in life, the psychic realm for instance. Instead of fleeing certain things that bother you like anger and sensuality, vanity, jealousy, etc., explore them, try to know them and see what they mean. The courage and audacity you will gain will also bring you the knowledge that the evil you took for an enemy was really a friend bearing gifts. The era is coming when mankind will adopt another attitude towards evil, it will learn by pedagogical methods the things that will bring liberation to all man's inner limitations."

I have already spoken a good deal on this subject: how man changed his attitude towards the forces of nature, water, air and electricity, and was then able to use them to accomplish extraordinary things. On the exterior there is no doubt that humans have won great victories over the elements; because it is always the outside world that is most important, they found the means and the methods to progress in that direction, and that's good. But the same danger, the same catastrophes threaten them in the inner life and yet this doesn't interest them, to them it is not important.

I often talk with young boys and girls who ask me questions on the subject of love, and none of them ever understand why physical relations can be harmful. On the contrary, for them that enjoyment and happiness will make them rich and healthy. But this is not so, and I try to explain why: All physiological manifestation is in the form of a combustion. When you think, when you speak, you are burning matter . . . which is even more true for your emotions. When you have a sudden great joy or a great sorrow, these are substances that burn and leave behind ashes and waste and diminution, from which the organism slowly recovers in sleep. Each manifestation, each emotion, each feeling, is at the cost of burned substance and energy. How can humans imagine that in the effervescence of love they spend nothing, they lose nothing? That is just where the cost is highest, where it is most difficult to recuperate. For these are quintessences of another nature, another quality, and in the long run the human being loses his beauty and intelligence and fineness.

This doesn't mean that everything must be repressed and you must live without love or tenderness. The thing is to live a sensible life which is both intelligent and esthetic. When you know that people wallow in physical pleasure with no attempt to include another element somewhat more spiritual, it is surprising and even shocking, because it is such a loss for them, such a great loss in every domain. It never occurs to humans that they might be losing something, for they think: "These organs don't wear out". It is true, those organs don't wear out, but in the brain, here in the brain, there is something that wears out. You have to know that. Love is good to the extent that it stimulates you and inspires you and gives you creative impulses, but if it does not, it is stupid. Most humans make love in the same way they sit down to a meal. They feel obliged to eat regularly, automatically, even if they feel nothing else.

I will repeat what I told a young girl who wanted to know what was right and what was wrong in connection with sex: is it better to live in chastity or to have sexual relations? I told her: "Actually that is not the way to put the question, but it is always put that way. Everyone has their opinion on what is good and what is bad. But that is not how to look at it. Those who choose to live in continence and chastity, are they in the right? It all depends on what is their goal. There can be bad results and there can be very good results. Continence makes some people hysterical, neurotic and ill, and it makes others strong, perfectly balanced and in sound health. Those who give free rein to all their instincts, are they right? They must have a reason. Can it do them good? Certainly, it can do a lot of good, but also a lot of harm. We should not classify things and say: 'This is good, that is bad'. Good and bad depend on another factor: how you use the forces, how you direct them. Nothing starts out good or bad, it becomes one way or the other.

"The whole question is to know first of all what your ideal is, what you wish to become. If you wish to become a soul, a spirit, an exceptional being, if you wish to make discoveries in the spiritual world and be in communication with Heaven, then you will be obliged to reduce the amount of pleasure or even give it up completely so as to learn to sublimate your sexual force. But if you haven't this high ideal, then it is idiotic to hold yourself back, to be chaste and virginal, and it will probably make you ill, because there is no sense in your efforts, there is no reason for them." Of course the young girl was astonished at my answer because no one had stated the problem in this way for her, either it was good, or it was bad. Is it wise to give the same advice, the same laws for everyone? Try asking a swine to remain virginal and chaste . . . he will look at you with surprise and say: "You're crazy! What kind of philosophy is that? Where did you come from?" Which is why I don't give the same advice to everyone.

Sometimes, someone will come to me and say: "O Maître, I don't think I should marry and have children, I feel that I am too spiritual." And when I see his constitution, his structure, I answer: "No, no, it is better for you to marry, otherwise it will be terrible, you will be unhappy and make everyone else unhappy." And when someone else tells me he wants to be married, sometimes I say: "Marry if you wish, but you should know that you are not made for marriage and you will be very unhappy." Lots of boys and girls don't know themselves at all and have no idea what they should do. Each person comes on earth with a mission, a programme to accomplish. It is not up to him to dispose of his tendencies and instincts as he wishes. I have told you: "Give a cat the best advice, tell him he should become vegetarian and give up eating mice ... he will agree, saying 'Miaou' in agreement. But while you are still preaching to him, there will be a small sound nearby, a little scratch, and off he goes, abandoning you with no regret, to catch the mouse. The mouse interests him more than your speeches. How is it possible to explain to humans who are cats that they mustn't eat mice?"

If you were to take a scale and put on one side everything to be gained by tasting every sensation, every excitement, every pleasure there is, and on the other side, everything we lose by giving in to them, you would see that you lose nearly everything and gain practically nothing. It is really not worth while sacrificing everything for nothing. But as one never thinks that feelings can be short-lived and forgotten (the food you ate yesterday can't nourish you today), one prepares for oneself a life of poverty. Whereas if you make the effort to refuse, you suffer for an instant, but you prepare a magnificent future for yourself. You may be giving up a few thrills, but you are gaining your entire future. The non-thinkers, the thoughtless say: "I am happy, I am so contented!" and they may be, but they have no future ahead of them. Take the case of a drunkard, it explains a whole philosophy: his pleasure is drinking, because wine makes him happy, he drinks wine. Yes, but later, if he keeps drinking, what will be the attitude of his boss, his family, his friends? The feeling he has is pleasant, but not for long. His future is in the gutter.

You are familiar with the Bible story about Esau selling his birthright to his brother Jacob for a platter of lentils. For a sensation, a feeling, a pleasure, he gave up his birthright and Jacob profited. This tale has never been properly interpreted. Most humans are very good at giving up the most valuable thing they own in exchange for a little pleasure; they are most adept at that, it's remarkable. But the disciple must learn to deprive himself of certain kinds of pleasure in order to acquire something else of greater value. Of course I am not saying that he should be deprived of everything all at once, it's up to him to know how, little by little, he can liberate himself from all that keeps him from the path of true evolution.

Do you think that those who have become great Masters spent their lives amidst pleasures and satisfactions? No, they lived in privation and self-denial and disgrace. But for them the future surpassed that of the most renowned princes, because they had chosen the path of self-denial. Most humans live in horror of self-denial, they don't wish to renounce a thing. They refuse to deprive themselves and insist on satisfying their every desire, their every need. Yes, but then their future presents itself very badly . . .

                                        Le Bonfin, July 31, 1975

The Need for a Guide

The young are always afraid they will be deprived of something they like. That's why they avoid all encounter with authority, with Masters . . . for fear of being prevented from being happy. They stick up for their own tastes and opinions and desires and projects, and that is why, later, many of them are unhappy and disappointed, after throwing themselves, with no experience to guide them, into all kinds of adventures that finish badly. Now, it must be explained to them that their fear is not justified, that no one wants to deprive them of joy or pleasure, on the contrary, we wish to show them how to have all the joy and pleasure without any harm to them, without damage and grief. To try and keep them from tasting natural joys is the height of stupidity. In the past, people who were neither psychologists nor educationalists, preached that it was better to live in privation and abstinence and absolute chastity, and this brought disastrous results.

You mustn't think that because you come to the Fraternity you must no longer eat or drink or get married and have children. The difference is that here we eat better, sleep better, marry more wisely, have better children. It's wonderful, we lack nothing except . . . all the nonsense. Of course if you need nonsense you can find that here too! So, this is what I would say to young people: considering that as yet you have no knowledge of human nature, you have never been through trouble, you think that everything is easy, when you begin to feel desire and instincts stirring within you, you won't know how to deal with them, how to act, and things will start going wrong for you. It is to avoid disaster that you need to be enlightened on certain subjects. "Yes, but now we're young and we don't feel like having to learn anything, it doesn't appeal to us." I know, I know, but you can't learn at the last minute. If you don't know anything, if you are totally unprepared, before you know it there will be a child. The mother will be some poor girl who is still a child herself, and she will tear her hair out and there will be two children instead of one. At that point, she will seek advice, but it's too late, she should have asked for instruction a little sooner. But no, the young don't want to learn, it doesn't appeal to them, they would rather play around and make fun of older people and leave their families in order to be free. And when their freedom works out badly, they go back to their parents – that is when they need their parents.

Youth needs to be guided, to be well directed and well instructed and well enlightened. What do they lose by listening to me? I have never deprived anyone of fun or pleasure, or stopped them from doing what they want to do, I only say that there is a better way to do everything and as they don't know how to do things better, they should come here to find out. Why oppose that, why be so obstinate and rebellious? I'll tell you why, it is because it is written in the destiny of those boys and girls that they need to suffer, that they must suffer. That is what pushes them to act that way, so as to suffer terribly. What will they lack here? Maybe a little ease and comfort, a few swimming pools and gambling dens and night clubs . . . but in two or three weeks, a month or so, they will be able to do without and it won't kill them, and they will be learning a great deal. Otherwise they will go on forever having fun without learning anything and in a short while, the pleasure to be derived from having fun will fade, they will be faced with more serious occupations, duties for which they are not prepared, because they will have spent their lives in distractions, and then they will tear out their hair.

That is what I want to say to the young: here they would be deprived of nothing, no one would stop them from anything, certainly not from loving and being loved, only they would be learning how to love. Of course, the usual love, love as it is understood in the world, everybody knows how to love that way, but there are higher degrees of love to know, and you must know them. I can see nothing but sorrow for those who refuse this knowledge and enlightenment. I am not clairvoyant, but I can see what is in store for someone from his way of reasoning, his behaviour, and what will happen to him is all too clear. I also say that when boys and girls obstinately refuse to listen to any advice, it is because they are inhabited by entities whose concern is to keep them from enlightenment, to keep them where they can feed on them. They may think they are free to choose and like this or that, but actually there are others inside who manifest their wishes through them. It is not they, but others who are expressing themselves across them, expressing their desires and feeding off them.

Let the young be unafraid, we will deprive them of nothing at all. There are some pretty little girls here aged fifteen who are dying for certain experiences. I say to them: "This is natural, there is nothing more normal, it's a wonderful experience to have, marvellous and holy and sacred, but I think it is just a little early, a little too soon, you must finish school and prepare yourselves ... marriage is a serious business. You will be deprived of nothing, you need only be patient for a little while." The others are the ones who are deprived, by not knowing enough to replace a stupid idea, an animal desire for which they will pay dearly, with ideas and desires and hopes that are better, on a higher level. It is they who will be unhappy. Everyone has his temperament, according to his nature he likes this or that and hates something else, it's natural, but if there is no intelligence present, bringing self-control, will-power, character, the Light, to direct and control and orient them in the right direction, then I know they are headed for a precipice. All these instincts and lusts are prehistoric tendencies, left over from prehistoric times. We have had them for thousands of years and they have brought us nothing but catastrophes, killing and war. Why always give way to our primitive nature without making certain there is something else in control which sees everything and directs us?

I will draw you a picture. You know what had to be done in the past to operate a ship. Below, in the ship's hold was the boiler room where the machinists, the men whose task was to feed the boilers worked, and because of them and their efforts, the ship moved forward, but they were not able to see the direction the ship took, that was the work of the captain on the bridge, who gave the orders and steered, but had nothing to do with making the ship move. It is the same with man: his emotions and feelings, his instincts, are the fuel he puts in the boiler to make him move, but if there is no one to steer, the ship will be dashed to pieces. During a cruise in the Arctic Ocean, a lady asked the captain: "What will happen if our ship hits an iceberg?" "Oh", answered the captain, "the iceberg will stay on course, ma'am." He didn't mention the ship because its fate was too obvious. The same thing happens with man. If he hits an iceberg, symbolically speaking, there is no need to talk about the outcome. The captain is here, in the head, and the men and engineers are in our stomach, sex, abdomen.

I say to young people: if you live only according to your wishes and desires and preferences, you will be sure to fall flat on your faces, because those impulses are blind. They may make life sweet and easy for the moment, but that is not the way to work towards the future that is waiting for you. It is vitally important to be both lucid and discerning, but these are qualities that come only with age, after many experiences. Therefore I say that you need someone to direct you, to keep you from foundering. Believe it or not, but I have seen it happen thousands of times. That you may have desires and impulses is understood, there is no doubt of that, each one of us is pushed on by instinctive forces, whether they come from our stomach, intestines, or sex, there is always something urging us on, but that is no reason to let ourselves go. If you remain ignorant you will of course enjoy many things, but your joy will soon change into suffering and bitterness and regret. An Initiate's joy is made of gold, pure gold. There is no need to give up all joy and all pleasure, but there is a need to recognize them for what they are, and to replace them with better joys and pleasures, purer and nobler and more beneficent.

I have not tried to keep people from being happy, as they did in the past when the religious, the Puritans, not knowing human nature very well, did more harm than good by imposing hardships and deprivation on people who couldn't bear it. You have to be a great psychologist and have a great knowledge of the way to teach in order to lead human beings. For thirty-eight years, I have been giving you a point of view that can never cause you any harm, if you understand it properly. Here you will never be deprived of anything at all, on the contrary, if you are in love, you will learn how to appreciate the one you love, how to hold him, otherwise you will never be able to hold him. You need to know a lot in order to protect your love, to sustain it and purify it and spiritualize it and make it holy. I am here to do precisely that, to teach you those things. I have done nothing all my life but experiment on things myself, to verify and replace and transform and sublimate, and it is thanks to these experiences that I can now be useful to you. But if you have no confidence in me, if you are afraid of being unhappy here, go ahead. I have nothing against your leaving, but it will be you who will suffer. One day you will see how stupid you were to behave that way, heedlessly, because you were blind to your own best interests.

My dear brothers and sisters, I say to you that nowhere will you be able to find a better friend than I. Sooner or later the others will leave you or refuse to see you when you need them most. Whereas I, I will always be here to receive you, to be useful to you and comfort you.

Le Bonfin, September 3, 1975

Youth and The Problem of Love
Give Your Love to
God First

Adolescents need to love other adolescents, to make exchanges, it is an indescribable need they can neither explain nor control. For years, doctors and psychologists have been studying their behaviour and even for them this whole question is not clear. In the light of Initiatic science we find the explanation.

Initiatic science teaches that the human being is made of several bodies: physical, astral, mental, etc. In the child, only the physical body expresses itself: he wants to eat and sleep and move around and feel things. Later, when he reaches the age of seven, his etheric body begins to express itself with his memory, his sensitivity to colour and odour, and to human manifestations. This period is the most important one for the rest of his life, because what he sees going on around him, what he hears, leaves an imprint on his etheric body, an imprint which will have a great bearing on his whole life. He may not yet entirely understand, his feelings are not as developed as those of an adult, but the child is sensitive, and everything he feels is imprinted on his consciousness. For this reason, those who live around children should take care not to expose them to terrible scenes, to scenes of violence or perversity that will mark them for life and from which they will suffer permanently despite all the help of doctors and psychiatrists.

When the child reaches fourteen, it is the astral body that

awakens: his emotions, his passionate feelings. But as the astral body is equally developed on the negative side as it is on the positive side, it manifests as much by the need to revolt and destroy as by the need to love. Of course he might show signs of attraction and repulsion before he is fourteen, but they will not be as strongly expressed. From the time he is fourteen, it is his feelings that dominate him, his feelings are his law and his driving power. When a boy or girl loves someone, you may give them every possible reason to make them change, but it will be useless, nothing doing, they would rather go on being guided by their feelings, they will not listen. Rather they rush headlong to find an outlet for their feelings, or, if they do listen and submit through fear or obedience or out of respect for their elders, inside they hold on to their feelings. Their feelings will always have the upper hand. When they reach twenty-one, the mental body awakens: thoughtfulness and reason are there to help the boy or girl dominate his feelings, to hold them back or diminish them, or perhaps to give them free rein, and let them express themselves.

But let's go back to the fourteenth year when the astral body awakens. Until then the child's tendency was to think only of himself, to take, to eat and drink and sleep and get dirty. Now if Cosmic Intelligence had not given man the need to have relationships with his fellow humans, he would have remained childish, permanently closed off in his corner with so much egoism that he would have brought about the extinction of the human race. That is why in his fourteenth year, a sense of the collectivity begins to stir: adolescents need to be together, to frequent each other and to know each other, they are affected by others, their faces and speech and actions. With the propagation of the species in mind, Cosmic Intelligence infused them with the need to meet and mingle, to dance together.

Yes, but the human error was to stop at the physical aspect, the biological aspect of this question, because that is not the whole plan. Cosmic Intelligence never intended man to have only a few little pleasures, to exchange a few caresses and kisses and gifts, and then start a little family. The plan was to lead humans toward a far more important, lofty and spiritual goal: the creation of the Universal White Brotherhood in the world. But as man's inferior nature has been for thousands of years more predominant than his superior nature, because he has always been badly advised and badly taught, his love has remained entirely personal, entirely selfish, always taking, possessing, dominating.

While they are still young and idealistic, some adolescents may not feel like going off alone with a boy or girl, they feel like loving the world, they need to embrace the entire world, but, after a while, because of the examples before them and because they have no one to guide them, they resign themselves to founding a little family, a family so selfish and so personal that it will keep the other Family, the universal Family from developing. In turn they teach their family to be selfish and narrow, against the collectivity, against Brotherhood, and this is the way the little family eventually destroys the large Family. But in the future, thanks to the knowledge and light of this Teaching that is handed down to us from above, there will be an expansion of the human consciousness, and men will be horrified to find that they have done nothing to contribute to the realization of the Kingdom of God and His Justice, the Golden Age, the great Universal White Brotherhood, which means freedom and happiness for the entire world.

This is why Cosmic Intelligence gave adolescents beginning at the age of fourteen, the need to expand and know others and make exchanges with each other. A young girl, should she wish to love the whole world, is told: "That's stupid, you're crazy." It is only stupid and crazy because she is still too young and weak to know that she will be sullied and devoured. It is really the others involved who are ignorant because instead of helping her to direct her impulse into the right channel, they don't take her seriously and then the impulse leaves, and is gone forever. As for a boy who thinks only of becoming a knight and being able to deliver the imprisoned and the oppressed, who wishes to consecrate his life to doing good, after a while, he too will have his head so full of what he is told that he gives up the rest to become "wise and sensible" and settle down.

If there were other people, Initiates, who could guide the young and their impulses, it would be the greatest blessing. That is why I advise young girls and boys who feel a divine urge, which is the greatest glory possible, to hide their feelings in front of idiots, otherwise it will all be ruined by so-called good advice. They should show nothing at all, but from time to time they should withdraw into themselves, and meditate on sending their love and their thoughts and their light throughout the whole world ... and wait for the moment when they will be able to manifest their love without danger on the physical plane, in the meanwhile sending their love to the higher regions. If they are in too much hurry to express their love physically, they will be destroyed by those who are not always careful, or reasonable, or well-intentioned. How many young boys have been "initiated" by an older woman who took advantage of their innocence and candour? How many cases of governesses who amused themselves by awakening sexual feelings in their little charges? But let's leave all that to the researches of psychiatrists.

For their good impulses not to be destroyed, I advise young people to give their impulses first to the invisible world, and then the spirits of Light will take charge of them. The spirits who watch and see everything, who work in the interests of preserving purity and light, will come to the aid of their impulses so they will not be lost and then the young will be able to see clearly and know when they can trust someone with their love, and when they should be wary. Nobody knows this unless they have been taught the Initiatic science, no teacher, no educator, no pedagogue, for the subject is too delicate! It is so important that our youth be guided by instructors who know what to teach them, and how to direct and orient their impulses.

Sèvres, January 25, 1976

Are Light, You Will Go Towards The Light' – 17. Everything has its Double - Making a New Recording – 18. Moral Law Becomes Entirely Significant in the Hereafter – 19. Example : the Best Method of Pedagogy – 20. 'Whosoever Shall Smite Thee on the One Cheek...' – 21. The New Year.

VOLUME 13 – A NEW EARTH
Methods, Exercices, Formulas and Prayers

1. Prayers – 2. A Daily Programme – 3. Nutrition – 4. Actions – 5. Overcoming the Evil in Us – 6. Methods of Purification – 7. Human Relations – 8. Man's Relations with Nature – 9. The Sun and the Stars – 10. Mental Work – 11. Spiritual Galvanoplasty – 12. The Solar Plexus – 13. The Hara Centre – 14. Methods for Working with Light – 15. The Aura – 16. The Body of Glory – 17. Formulas and Prayers.

VOLUME 14 – LOVE AND SEXUALITY – PART I

1. The Masculine and Feminine Principles - The Love of God, the Love of Others, Self Love – 2. Taking the Bull by the Horns - The Caduceus of Mercury – 3. The Serpent - Isis Unveiled – 4. The Power of the Dragon – 5. Spirit and Matter – The Sexual Organs – 6. Manifestations of the Masculine and Feminine Principles – 7. Jealousy – 8. The Twelve Doors of Man – 9. From Yesod to Kether : The Path of Sexual Sublimation – 10. The Spiritual Screen – 11. Nourishment and Love – 12. Woman's Role in the New Culture – 13. The Initiatic Meaning of Nudity – 14. Exchanges and Relationships – 15. Wealth and Poverty – 16. To Love is the Work of the Disciple – 17. Love in the Universe – 18. A Wider Concept of Marriage I – 19. The Twin-Soul – 20. Everything Depends on Your Point of View – 21. A Wider Concept of Marriage II and III – 22. Analysis and Synthesis – 23. Like the Sun, Love Brings Order to Life – 24. Mother Love – 25. The Meaning of Renunciation – 26. The Bonds of Love – 27. Youth and the Problem of Love - The New Currents - Marriage - Why Self-Control - The Need for a Guide - Give Your Love to God First.

VOLUME 15 – LOVE AND SEXUALITY – PART II

1. A Question of Attitude – 2. True Marriage – 3. The Sun is the Source of Love – 4. The Goal of Love is Light – 5. The Manifestations of the Masculine and Feminine Principles – 6. Master or Mistress ? – 7. Vestal Virgins ; the New Eve – 8. Materialism, Idealism and Sexuality - 'On Earth as in Heaven' – 9. Heart and Mind ; the Universal White Brotherhood – 10. Seek the Soul and the Spirit – 11. Restoring Love to its Pristine Purity – 12. Love Transforms Matter – 13. Love and Identification – 14. The Task of a Disciple – 15. Open Yourself to Others and They Will Love You – 16. Tantra-Yoga – 17. Emptiness and Fullness : the Holy Grail – 18. Love is Everywhere – 19. Look for Love at its Source – 20. Know How to Use Your Powers of Love – 21. A Broader Concept of Marriage, Part IV – 22. It Rises

By the same author :
(translated from the French)

Izvor Collection

PRINTED IN FRANCE IN MARCH 1989
EDITIONS PROSVETA Z.I. DU CAPITOU
B.P.12 – 83601 FRÉJUS CEDEX
FRANCE

– N° d'impression : 1685 –
Dépôt légal : Mars 1989
Printed in France